Creative Paper Jewelry

EARRINGS, PENDANTS, BEADS & PINS

DAFNA YAROM

sixth&spring
books

CONTENTS

sixth&spring
books

Copyright © 2010 by Sixth&Spring Books
161 Avenue of the Americas
New York, NY 10013
sixthandspringbooks.com

Produced for Sixth&Spring Books by
Penn Publishing Ltd.
www.penn.co.il

Editor: Shoshana Brickman
Design and layout: Michal & Dekel
Photography: Roee Feinburg
Styling: Roni Chen
Makeup artist: Perry Halfon

Catalog-in-Publication data is available
upon request.
ISBN-13: 978-1-936096-06-0
Library of Congress Control Number:
2010921210

Manufactured in China
1 3 5 7 9 10 8 6 4 2
First Edition

INTRODUCTION

Paper is, in its essence, a changeable, malleable material, open to endless possibilities for expression and creativity. It can be thin or thick, stiff or flexible, textured or smooth, patterned or plain. Paper is stunning in a range of colors and beautiful in a single shade. It can convey light or mask it, and be modeled into diverse items of every size and dimension.

Paper is an excellent material for making handmade jewelry, since it allows you to create objects in diverse shapes, textures and colors and to give life to your imagination. By combining handmade paper pieces with ribbons, beads, chains and diverse metal components, you can make unique necklaces, earrings and brooches that are ornate or simple, sophisticated or lighthearted. Paper jewelry also provides an unusual medium for using beautiful papers, giving them an additional life you may never have imagined.

Creative Paper Jewelry contains dozens of projects (and even more visual examples) for transforming this recyclable, environmentally friendly material into unique, contemporary and highly personalized pieces of jewelry.

Many of the projects are made with components that were salvaged from old pieces of jewelry such as gold-plated chains, rhinestone-inlaid shells and earring backs. So, in addition to reusing and recycling paper, you'll also learn how to give new life to old pieces of jewelry. This adds a sentimental element to the pieces, as well.

"With imagination and instruction, paper's qualities can be adapted to create jewelry in every shape, size and style," says Dafna. "I hope every reader discovers how paper can become an expression of his or her own imagination and style."

About the Author

Dafna Yarom embarked on her love affair with paper more than twenty years ago. "For me," Dafna says, "the thrill of working with paper lies in the ability to create unique, fresh, modern jewelry using materials available to everyone. The jewelry can be bold and playful, elegant and delicate. There's no limit. Paper can inspire, and it can be an expression of inspiration."

As part of her degree work in graphic design at the prestigious Bezalel Academy of Arts and Design in Jerusalem, Dafna Yarom participated in a handmade paper workshop. After continuing to study papermaking in Japan, she began to explore paper-based arts, including paper drawings, paper light sculptures, cardboard furniture and, of course, paper jewelry. Her works have appeared in exhibitions and galleries throughout Israel.

MATERIALS

Paper, Paper, Paper

All of the projects in this book use one or more types of paper. Some papers are used to make the base of the paper piece; others are used as the top layer. All of these papers are described below.

Base Papers

The type of paper you use for the base may determine the width and texture of your paper piece. It may also be a deciding factor in the type of top layer you choose. For instance, if your base is made with newspaper-based paper pulp, it will be visible in the finished piece if you choose light-colored paper as a top layer. Keep this in mind when selecting the paper for your base.

Bristol board is a relatively heavy paper that can be used to form the base of paper pieces. It usually has a smooth finish and comes in a variety of weights. Bristol board can also be used to cover a paper base before applying the top layer. Use it to make a hilly surface by layering small pieces of Bristol board in various sizes.

Computer paper can be used to make paper pulp with a smooth consistency. It can also be used to cover corrugated cardboard or Bristol board bases, and it provides a neutral surface for applying paint or paper covering.

Corrugated cardboard is the material used to make boxes. It usually consists of one fluted corrugated sheet sandwiched between two flat liner boards. Corrugated cardboard comes in various weights and thicknesses. It is a great base for paper pieces, since the fluted interior serves nicely as a ready-made tunnel for stringing your paper piece. (Fig. 1)

Newspaper can be used to make paper pulp or to cover cardboard and Bristol board bases. Newspaper is plentiful, but it has the drawback of being colored with ink. This means it produces grayish paper pulp. If you use newspaper to make your base, make sure the top layer is dark.

Toilet paper can be used to make paper pulp that is light in color and has a feathery consistency. It can also be wrapped around wire to make paper beads.

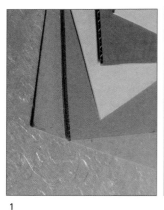

1   2   3   4

Top Layer

Use any type of beautiful paper you like for the top layer of your paper piece. Paper comes in countless textures, colors, hues and shapes. You can use scraps of paper you have saved from cards, presents or packages. You can also use paper you picked up in bazaars, markets or specialty paper shops. Paper is available in hobby shops and craft stores, as well as office supply stores and gift shops.

Batik paper is vibrantly colored paper made by dipping knotted washi paper in dye. It is inspired by traditional batik fabric design. (Fig. 2)

Decorative paper napkins are available in an endless variety of prints, designs, colors and sizes. They are easy to find in kitchen stores, art supply stores and online. Most decorative napkins have several layers, but only the top layer is decorated. This is the layer you'll be using for your work. (The other layers can be used to make paper pulp.) (Fig. 3)

Handmade paper comes in a wide variety of styles. It may be made from rags, straw, bark, wood, vegetables or other fibrous materials. There are dozens of companies worldwide that sell handmade paper. There are also online tutorials for making handmade paper yourself.

Origami paper is Japanese paper that comes in various square dimensions. The standard size is 6 x 6" (15 x 15 cm). Made of long fibers, it is strong, flexible, dense and thin. Origami paper comes in a vast assortment of colors and traditional Japanese prints. (Fig. 4)

Washi paper is a type of thin handmade paper from Japan, also known as wagami or rice paper. Made in a traditional manner from a variety of trees and grasses, it has a wonderful texture. Washi comes in a wide variety of colors, patterns and textures and may contain materials such as dried leaves and flowers, or sprinkles of gold and silver dust. Washi paper can become doughy when brushed with PVA glue, so apply it sparingly.

Other Materials

♕

In addition to paper, a wide variety of other materials are used to make the projects in this book. They range from strips of wood to plastic beads, from jewelry adhesive to wire. If you don't have the material specified in a certain project, feel free to make substitutions.

Beads are included in almost every project in this book. These include glass beads, crystal beads, plastic beads, wooden beads and metallic beads. If you like, substitute some or all of the beads specified with beads you have on hand. Of course, feel free to vary the colors I suggest as well. When selecting beads that will be strung on ribbon, make sure their holes are large enough to fit over the ribbon but small enough to stay in place after the beads are strung.

Chains are used in abundance in these projects. A variety of gold-plated and silver-plated chains are used for stringing beads and adding decoration. Though chains are sold at beading and jewelry stores, I often salvage chains from old pieces of jewelry, purse handles, belts and other items. For chains with unsoldered links, open the links with pliers to divide the chain into pieces. For chains with soldered links, cut the links with wire cutters. (Page 10, Fig. 1)

Elastic gold cord is used as stringing material. It is a sparkling way of stringing your paper pieces. (Page 10, Fig. 2)

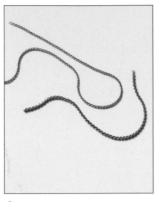

1 2 3 4

Fabric hardener is a slow-drying fiber hardener. When brushed on paper, it causes the paper to harden and hold its shape permanently. Fabric hardener is available in a variety of colors; choose transparent hardener to maintain the original look of your paper. For more about using fabric hardener, see page 16.

Glitter glue is painted on pieces to give a shiny, sparkly finish.

Jewelry adhesive is a high-performance glue that is perfect for affixing decorated paper pieces to metal, plastic or other materials. I recommend using a slow-drying adhesive so that you have time to position items exactly as you want them before the glue dries.

Jewelry findings are the items that hold your pieces of jewelry together. Be sure to select high-quality findings since the longevity of your jewelry depends on it.

• Bead caps are decorative additions placed on either side of a bead to dress it up a bit. (Fig. 3)

• Clasps are used to connect necklaces. There come in an endless variety, and I simply suggest choosing one that suits the design of the necklace. (Fig. 4)

• Clip-on earrings can be used to make earrings for women who do not have pierced ears.

• Cord tips are used to seal cord ends and to provide a loop for attaching jump rings and clasps. (Fig. 5)

• Crimp beads are used to hold chains in place. They are flattened with flat-nose pliers.

• Ear wires are used to make earrings for pierced ears. They often have loops at one end, for stringing decorative elements. (Fig. 6)

• Eye pins are used to make dangling beads and to string paper objects. They have a loop at the base. (Fig. 7)

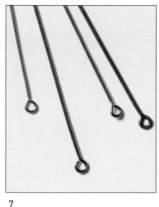

5   6   7   8

- Head pins are used to make dangling beads and to string paper objects. They have a flat base. (Fig. 8)

- Jump rings are used to connect jewelry parts. Be sure to select unsoldered jump rings, since you'll need to open and close them.

- Tube beads are used to decorate necklace ribbons and to connect pendants to the ribbon. (Page 12, Fig. 9)

Leather cord is used to string paper pieces and beads.

Metallic dust adds a sparkling touch to paper pieces. It comes in a variety of colors, including gold, silver and copper.

Needles are used to sew up ribbon ends and pierce holes. Use ordinary sewing needles to sew and thick embroidery needles for piercing holes.

Plastic containers are used for mixing paints, as well as storing paper pulp, diluted PVA glue and metallic dust mixture.

Plastic wrap protects your work surface when working with fabric hardener. It is also used to wrap paper pulp beads when shaping them so that the pulp doesn't stick to your fingers.

PVA (Polyvinyl acetate) glue, also known as white glue, is used in many projects. Select PVA glue that is highly concentrated, dries transparent and will not turn yellow.

- Diluted PVA glue is made by combining water and PVA glue at a ratio of 2 tablespoons of water for every 1 tablespoon of glue. Mix well until smooth then apply with a paintbrush. It is used to affix paper pieces smoothly onto surfaces.

Ribbons of various types and styles are used to make the necklaces in this book. You can use the one specified in the project or substitute a ribbon you prefer. When using delicate ribbons such as organdy, make sure you slide the beads on gently, so as not to cut or fray the ribbons.
(Page 12, Fig. 10)

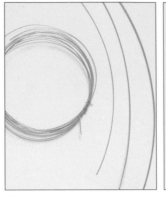
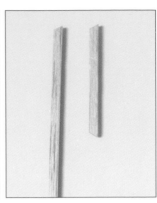

9   10   11   12

Sandpaper is used to smooth the edges of cut wood.

Thread is used to sew ribbon ends together.

Varnish is brushed on paper items to protect them and provide a smooth finish. Matte varnish is best for preserving the paper's texture; glossy varnish accentuates the colors. Some projects call for **gloss glaze,** which produces a glazed finish. Select the varnish you prefer for your projects.

Wire

- Brass wire is used to string beads and paper pieces that are too large to be strung onto standard eye pins or head pins. I usually use 24-gauge (0.5 mm) wire. (Fig. 11)

- Nickel silver wire, also known as alpaca, is used to string paper pieces that are too large to be strung onto standard eye pins or head pins. It is also used to string beads with very small holes, as decoration and to tie components together.

- Tie wire supports paper bases as you work on them and forms a tunnel for stringing paper pieces once they are decorated. Sold in building supply stores and online, it comes in various widths or gauges. I prefer using 19-gauge (0.9 mm) wire. Tie wire can be replaced with other galvanized wires; just make sure the wire you choose leaves behind a hole that is wide enough for stringing.

Wood rods are used to make dangling origami-covered beads. Cut them with a utility knife or small saw.

Wood strips made from balsa wood are lightweight and easy to cut with a utility knife. They can be replaced with other types of wood strips. (Fig. 12)

TOOLS

Transforming paper into jewelry requires simple tools such as scissors, paintbrushes, wire cutters and pliers. All of the tools used in this book are easy to find online or in hobby shops and hardware stores.

Compass You can use this to make perfect circles. You can also use a cup, saucer or bowl if it is just the right size.

Cutting mat Use this to protect your work surface when cutting with a utility knife. You can substitute a sheet of durable material, such as rubber, if you like. (Fig. 1)

Metalwork file This is used to smooth sharp metal edges.

Paintbrushes Use these to apply fabric hardener, glue, varnish and paint. Be sure to select high quality brushes that won't shed their bristles. (Fig. 2)

Pliers Several different types of pliers are used in these projects.

- <u>Flat-nose</u> pliers are used to open and close jump rings and links and to flatten crimp beads and cord tips. (Fig. 3)

- <u>Punch pliers</u> are used to punch holes in thick paper.

1

2

3

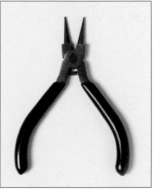
4

- <u>Round-nose pliers</u> are used to make loops in head pins, eye pins and pieces of wire and to open and close jump rings and links. (Page 13, Fig. 4)

Saw Use a small saw to cut small pieces of wood.

Scissors Make sure you have a sharp pair on hand for cutting paper, thread and other materials.

Support stand You'll need a base to support your paper piece as you work on it. You can use a piece of cork, a Styrofoam block or anything else into which you can insert a piece of wire. (Fig. 5)

Utility knife This is used to cut paper and other materials with precision. (Fig. 6)

Wire cutters These are used to cut brass, nickel silver and tie wire. (Fig. 7)

5

6

7

TIPS

As you gain experience working with paper, you'll find it easier to achieve the effects that you want. Be patient, curious and ready to experiment. I'm sure you'll be delighted with the things you discover. Reread the tips below as you work your way through the projects, since some tips may be more relevant to certain projects.

Let the paper lead the way

The jewelry I make is often led by the paper I use to make it. I love paper that is visually and sensually beautiful, and I usually let the paper lead the project. I hope that by learning the techniques in this book, you'll have the freedom to do the same.

Work your way up

Paper is widely available and comes in a range of prices. This means you can start by using less expensive paper and when you feel confident with the technique, select a more expensive paper.

Experiment!

Don't be afraid to try out new ideas! For example, after you have made a few symmetrical pieces, try your hand at making asymmetrical ones. And if you make a mistake along the way, don't worry. You can learn a lot from mistakes. You may even be surprised when what seems to be a mistake becomes the inspiration for a new piece.

Fixing mistakes is easy

If a paper base turns out all wrong, try fixing it with paper pulp or another layer of paper. If it still isn't right, throw it away and try again. After all, the basic materials you are working with are plentiful and inexpensive

Start saving paper

Many people collect paper for their recycling box. If you aren't already used to saving paper, now is the time to start. Save leftover decorative paper napkins, tissue paper, wrapping paper, colored paper, craft paper and handmade paper cards. These are all excellent sources of paper for using to make paper jewelry. Collect them in a large box and sort through them for inspiration.

Use paper wisely

Handmade paper and washi paper can be costly, so don't let it go to waste. When covering an object with this type of paper, try positioning the object in a corner of the paper rather than the center so that the excess paper you cut away is large enough to use for another project.

Tear off straight edges

Make sure there are no straight edges on the paper you used for covering the base, or for the top layer. Using paper with torn edges helps you achieve a smoother and more uniform result and improves the adherence between the pieces and layers.

Crumple base papers

When applying paper to cover the base, crumple it before spreading it with PVA glue. The paper fibers will absorb the PVA glue more efficiently if they are crumpled.

Adjust the number of paper layers as desired

Applying more layers results in a thicker, bulkier finished piece; applying fewer layers results in a thinner, more delicate piece. For an interesting artistic surface, vary the layers used on different areas of the base.

Reuse jewelry components

I love "discovering" new beads and components by taking apart old pieces of jewelry. My friends and family know I love jewelry that's no longer in style, so they often supply me with raw materials by donating old earrings, necklaces and bracelets.

Add a sentimental touch

Try integrating a component of old jewelry that has sentimental value. You'll find that the new item resonates with meaning, too.

Be creative!

Attaching gemstones, crystals, metal components and other items to handmade paper pieces often produces attractive, artistic and unique results. Even inexpensive plastic beads can give a piece that special touch. The projects in this book are meant to serve as a guide. Once you start integrating diverse materials into your work, you'll find that your sources are unlimited. Use your imagination and don't be afraid to experiment. I'm sure you'll be delighted both with the process and the results!

A Few Words about Fabric Hardener

When using transparent fabric hardener, read the manufacturer's instructions carefully and follow them to the letter. Cutting corners can mar the quality of your finished product. Fabric hardener can dim the shine of gold paper, so if your paper has gold decorations or printing on one side, apply fabric hardener on the other side ONLY. You'll need to apply a thicker layer of hardener on this side. As a general rule, fabric hardener should be shaken before use.

Place the paper you are covering on a large piece of plastic and brush one side with the fabric hardener. Let it dry until it is no longer sticky but still moist. Lift the paper, turn it over and place it on a clean area of the plastic. Brush this side with the hardener. Let it dry until this side is no longer sticky but still moist.

You now have about two hours to sculpt the paper as you like. The paper will harden as it dries completely and your piece will attain its permanent shape.

A washi-covered cardboard base enhanced with crystal beads, this pendant is a variation of the Glamorous Hoop Pendant (page 45) and the Fanciful Fairy Necklace (page 82).

BASIC TECHNIQUES

This section introduces you to several techniques for making paper pieces. All of the projects in the book refer to specific techniques, but most of these are interchangeable. You can choose any technique that appeals to you. Try them all, see which ones work best for you and enjoy!

Paper Pulp

Paper pulp can be used to form beads of any shape or size you like. You can also use it to build an interesting surface on Bristol board or cardboard bases, paper bases and other materials. Ready-made paper pulp can be purchased at some art supply stores, but it's easy to make at home using toilet paper, computer paper or newspaper.

NOTE When working with paper pulp, moisturize your hands often with hand cream. This helps prevent the pulp from sticking to your fingers. Also, since you'll probably wash your hands frequently when working with paper pulp, it helps prevent your hands from becoming dry.

If you find it difficult to work with your paper pulp, it may be too sticky. Try placing the paper pulp on a flat work surface and letting it dry out a bit. Once it is less sticky, it will be easier to mold. Items made with paper pulp are very forgiving. If you don't like the shape of the object after it dries, simply add a bit more pulp, smooth it with PVA glue and let it dry.

If you want to make a light-colored paper piece, use white paper (such as white toilet paper or computer paper) for your paper pulp.

Paper pulp made with printed paper, such as newspaper, has a dark grayish color and is fine when you will be using opaque paper for the top layer. If you don't want this color to be visible in the finished piece, cover it with one or two layers of computer paper or paint on a coat of white acrylic paint.

Paper pulp can be stored for several days. Simply wrap it in plastic or place it in a sealed container and store it in the refrigerator.

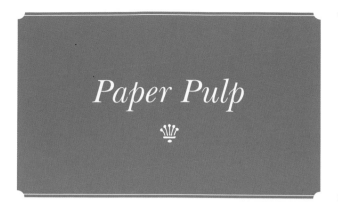

Paper Pulp

Paper pulp can be used to make a wide variety of pieces and can be covered with a top layer that is light or transparent. If you need only a small amount of paper pulp, I suggest using white tissue or toilet paper; since this type of paper has no glue, it dissolves easily.

MATERIALS

7 cups hot water

About 16" (5m) white toilet paper, torn into 1" (2.5 cm) pieces

PVA glue

TOOLS

Large bowl

Wooden spoon

Immersion blender

Strainer

Plastic wrap

Plastic container, for storage

DIRECTIONS

1. Pour the hot water into a bowl. Stir in the torn paper, using your hands or a wooden spoon to break it up. Blend the mixture with an immersion blender until it attains a feathery texture.

2. Press the mixture through a strainer to remove the water. Use your hands to squeeze out any remaining liquid. Mix in about 8 tablespoons of PVA glue. Knead until the mixture becomes doughlike and feels consistent and flexible. It should be a bit sticky.

3. Place the mixture in a container, cover with plastic wrap and let it rest overnight. The mixture will be ready for molding after about 12 hours.

NOTE You can also make paper pulp with used computer paper, newspapers or scraps of Bristol board. Note that making pulp this way can result in a pulp with a grayish tint. If you want to avoid this, choose pieces of paper that don't have too much print on them or rip away the printed areas.

Bristol Board Base

♕

In this technique, you'll sandwich a piece of tie wire between two pieces of Bristol board. Cut the board in any shape you like. If you want a symmetrical paper piece, make sure you position the wire down the middle of the shape. Of course, you can use this technique to make paper pieces of any shape.

MATERIALS

Bristol board, 2- or 3-ply
PVA glue
Tie wire, 19-gauge (0.9 mm)
Petroleum jelly
Diluted PVA glue
Computer paper or newspaper, straight edges torn away

TOOLS

Pencil
Compass
Utility knife
Cutting mat
Wire cutters
Support stand
Paintbrush

DIRECTIONS

1. Fold the Bristol board in half and draw the desired shape on one side. Cut both sides of the board at the same time to make two identical shapes. Brush PVA glue on one side of one shape.

2. Cut a piece of tie wire that is about 4" (10 cm) longer than the shape you want to make. The extra length will extend from the top and bottom of the shape. You'll use it to handle the shape while applying the base cover and decorating. Make an S-shaped bend in the bottom third of the wire. This "S" helps support the shape as you work on it.

3. Lubricate the area above the "S" with petroleum jelly, then place this part of the tie wire across the center of the glued side of the shape, with the wire extending evenly on both sides of the shape.

NOTE The hole made by the tie wire will be used later for stringing the shape, so make sure the wire is oriented in the right direction and located in the exact center of the shape.

1   2   3

4. Brush PVA glue on the other shape and place it on top of the first, glued sides together, sandwiching the tie wire between them. Press the two sides together firmly to affix. (Fig. 1)

5. Insert the bottom end of the wire into the support stand. Set aside until the glue dries. Tear the computer paper into small pieces measuring about ¾ x ¾" (2 x 2 cm) and crumple the pieces.

6. Brush diluted PVA glue on one side of the shape. Brush diluted PVA glue on both sides of a piece of computer paper or newspaper and affix the paper to the base. Rub the paper lightly after it has been affixed, with either your fingertips or a paintbrush, to remove air bubbles and fasten it securely to the base.

7. Repeat Step 6 until one face of the paper base is completely covered with paper. Remember to use narrower pieces when wrapping the edge of the base, for a smoother look. To create

a narrower edge and thicker mid-section, apply 3 or 4 layers of paper to the face of the base, and just 1 layer to cover the edge. The irregular surface contributes to the artistic uniqueness of the piece. Wrap the paper pieces around the tie wire, taking care to leave an opening. (Figs. 2 and 3)

8. Using your fingers, brush diluted PVA glue across the face to smooth out air bubbles. Let dry using the support stand.

9. Repeat Steps 6 to 8 on the other side of the base. Let dry. Do not flatten the surface as it dries, allowing it to form into a slightly curved, seemingly fluid shape. It it becomes too wavy, you can flatten it when it's dry. If you'd like a thicker shape, apply more layers of paper using the technique described above.

10. Decorate the shape as desired, or as described in the project instructions. When the decorated shape is dry, gently pull out the tie wire.

Corrugated Cardboard Base

With this technique, the tie wire is inserted into one of the waves in the middle of the cardboard. For a thicker (or thinner) paper piece, use thicker (or thinner) cardboard. If you don't plan on stringing the base onto a wire (for example, when making a base that will be connected with a chain or jump ring), there is no need to use tie wire.

MATERIALS

Corrugated cardboard, about ⅛" (3 mm) thick

Tie wire, 19-gauge (0.9 mm)

Petroleum jelly

Computer paper or newspaper, straight edges torn away

Diluted PVA glue

PVA glue

TOOLS

Pencil

Compass

Utility knife

Cutting mat

Wire cutters

Support stand

Paintbrush

DIRECTIONS

1. Draw the desired shape on the corrugated cardboard and cut.

2. Cut a piece of tie wire that is about 4" (10 cm) longer than the shape you want to make. The extra length will extend from the top and bottom of the shape. You'll use it to handle the shape while applying the base cover and decorating.

3. Make an S-shaped bend in the bottom third of the wire. This "S" helps support the shape as you work on it.

4. Lubricate the area above the "S" with petroleum jelly; then insert this part of the wire into the center wave in the cardboard.

NOTE When this wire is removed, it will leave a tunnel for stringing the paper piece. If you want the tunnel in the center of the base, be sure to insert the wire into the center wave.

1

2

3

4

5. Insert the tie wire into the support stand and let dry.

6. Tear the computer paper or newspaper into small pieces measuring about ¾ x ¾" (2 x 2 cm) and crumple the pieces.

7. Brush diluted PVA glue on one side of the shape. Brush diluted PVA glue on both sides of a piece of computer paper and affix it to the base. Rub the paper lightly after it has been affixed, either with your fingertips or a paintbrush, to remove air bubbles and fasten it securely to the base. (Fig. 1)

8. Repeat Step 7 until one face of the shape is covered with paper. Remember to use narrower pieces when wrapping the edge of the base, for a smoother look. Wrap the paper pieces around the tie wire, taking care to leave an opening.

9. Using your fingers, brush diluted PVA glue across the face to smooth out air bubbles. Let dry using the support stand. (Fig. 2)

10. Repeat Steps 7 to 9 on the other side of the base. If you'd like a thicker shape, apply more layers of paper using the technique described above. (Figs. 3 and 4)

11. Decorate the shape as desired, or as described in the project instructions. When the decorated shape is dry, gently pull out the tie wire.

NOTE To create a thinner edge and thicker mid-section, apply 3 or 4 layers of paper to the face of the disk and use just 1 layer to wrap the edge. The irregular surface contributes to the artistic uniqueness of the piece.

Paper Pulp Bead

The instructions below are for making an oval bead. By adjusting your molding technique, you can follow the same steps to make round, square, rectangular or asymmetrical beads. I recommend making several beads at a time in various shapes and sizes.

MATERIALS

Paper pulp (page 19)
Plastic wrap, 6 x 6" (15 x 15 cm)
Tie wire, 19-gauge (0.9 mm)
Petroleum jelly

TOOLS

Support stand

DIRECTIONS

1. Shape about ½ tablespoon of paper pulp into a ball. Wrap the ball with plastic wrap and then shape it with your fingers to form an oval. Pull away one side of the plastic wrap and place the shape, with the plastic wrap underneath it, on a flat surface. Smooth the surface of the oval using the free flap of the plastic wrap, then let the shape sit for about 1 to 2 hours, with the plastic wrap under it, until it dries somewhat. You'll know you're ready for the next step when the surface is less sticky and a bit harder. (Fig. 1)

2. Cut a piece of tie wire that is about 4" (10 cm) longer than the shape you want to make. The extra length will extend from the top and bottom of the shape. You'll use it to handle the bead while decorating. Make an S-shaped bend in the bottom third of the wire. This "S" helps support the shape as you work on it.

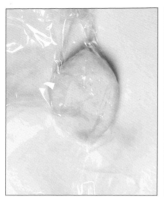

1

2

3. Lubricate the area above the "S" with petroleum jelly; then insert the wire through the center of the oval shape, orienting it in the desired direction. (Fig. 2)

NOTE The hole made by the tie wire will be used later for stringing the bead, so make sure the wire is oriented in the right direction and located in the exact center of the bead.

4. Set the bead aside to dry a bit more.

5. When the bead hardens and the surface is no longer sticky, remove the plastic wrap and insert the tie wire into the support stand. Set aside to dry completely. This may take more than 24 hours.

6. Decorate the shape as desired, or as described in the project instructions. When the decorated shape is dry, gently pull out the tie wire.

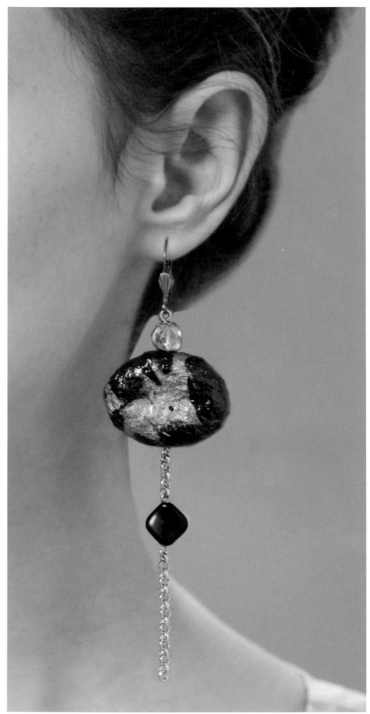

Concave Paper Shell

With this technique, paper pulp is sculpted into a rounded, concave, shell-like shape. After the shell is completely dry, holes for stringing it onto a piece of wire or chain can be made using a needle.

MATERIALS

Paper pulp (page 19)
Plastic wrap, 6 x 6" (15 x 15 cm)
PVA glue

TOOLS

Paintbrush

DIRECTIONS

1. Shape about ½ tablespoon of paper pulp into a ball with a ¾" (2 cm) diameter.

2. Place the ball on a corner of the plastic wrap and hold it in the palm of your hand. Fold the rest of the plastic over the ball to cover the top of it.

3. Using your finger, make gentle circular motions, pressing into the center of the ball (the area covered with plastic wrap) to make the shape concave. (Fig. 1)

4. When you're satisfied with the shape, gently remove the top part of the plastic wrap to expose the pulp to the air. Using a paintbrush or your finger, brush a bit of PVA glue over the surface of the concave area to make it smooth. Set aside until it is partially dry.

1

5. Pinch the edges of the shape with your fingers to make them even thinner. If the pulp is still a bit sticky, place the plastic wrap over the edge as you work. Press in the bottom as well, sculpting as desired while pulling up the edges using the plastic wrap.

6. Modify the shape if you like, adding more paper pulp as required and smoothing the surface with PVA glue. When you're satisfied with the shape, set aside (on the plastic wrap) to dry completely.

7. Decorate the shape as desired, or as described in the project instructions.

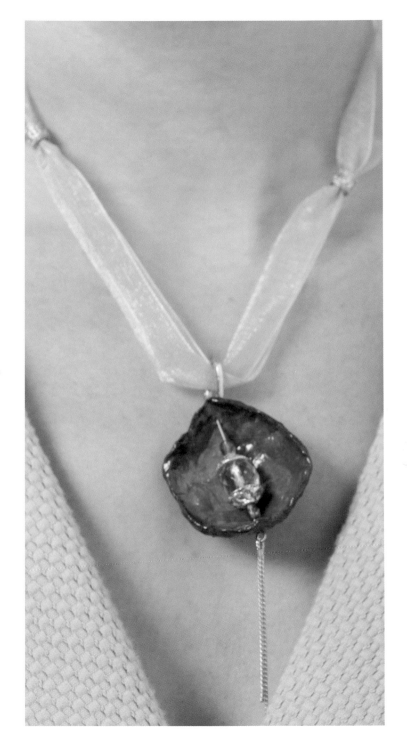

Sculpted Paper Beads

This simple technique can be used to make paper beads of any size or shape. I recommend using toilet paper to make these beads, since it is readily available, easily absorbs the glue and can be painted any color you like.

MATERIALS

Tie wire, 19-gauge (0.9 mm)
Petroleum jelly
Toilet paper
PVA glue
Paper pulp (page 19), optional

TOOLS

Support stand
Paintbrush

DIRECTIONS

1. Cut a piece of tie wire that is about 4" (10 cm) longer than the shape you want to make. The extra length will extend from the top and bottom of the shape. You'll use it to handle the shape while applying the base cover and decorating. Lubricate the area where you plan to make your bead with petroleum jelly.

2. Fold a strip of toilet paper about 4 times in one direction, until it is about 1" (2.5 cm) wide.

3. Wrap the toilet paper around the wire once and brush with PVA glue to secure. (Fig. 1)

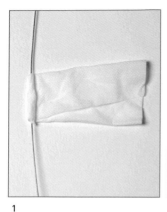

1 2 3 4

4. Make an S-shaped bend in the bottom third of the wire, directly below the area where the toilet paper is wrapped. This "S" will support the bead as you work on it. Continue wrapping the toilet paper around the wire for about 7 rotations, brushing with PVA glue every 2 rotations. Move from the top of the shape to the bottom as you wrap, forming an X pattern with the paper, so that the middle is thicker than the ends. Affix the ends of the paper. (Fig. 2)

5. Brush a generous amount of PVA glue over the entire surface of the shape. Knead until the glue is absorbed thoroughly and the paper becomes flexible. Mold the piece to attain the desired shape. (Fig. 3)

6. Gently brush a thin layer of PVA glue on the surface, smoothing it until the surface is uniform. Set aside to partially dry using the support stand. You'll know you're ready for the next stage when the surface is less sticky and a bit harder.

7. Modify the shape as you like by adding pulp and smoothing with glue. Let dry completely.

8. Decorate the shape as desired, or as described in the project instructions. (Fig. 4)

9. When the decoration is dry, gently pull the tie wire out of the piece.

This sculpted paper bead is perfectly framed by a gold-plated chain and a round pearly bead. (see Golden Galaxy Necklace, pages 66-69)

Making a Viewfinder

This easy-to-make tool helps you select the section of decorative paper you'll use to cover your paper piece. Simply cut out a hole in a sheet of computer paper that is the same size as the paper piece you want to cover. Move the computer paper over the decorative paper until you zoom in on just the right section of paper.

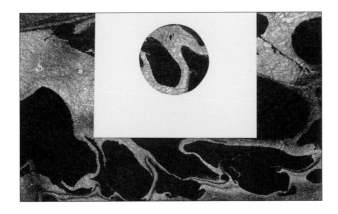

Embellishing with Decorative Paper

MATERIALS

Decorative paper
Paper base to be covered
Diluted PVA glue

TOOLS

Viewfinder
Pencil
Scissors
Paintbrush
Support stand

Make the very most of a piece of beautiful decorative paper by using it to cover a handmade paper piece. Select the section of paper you use carefully so that you choose an area that really enhances your paper piece. If possible, choose a section that's near one edge of the decorative paper, so that you maximize your use of the paper.

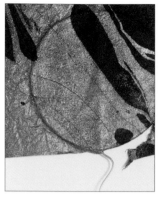
1

2

DIRECTIONS

1. Determine the size of the decorative paper you'll need to cover the base. In general, I recommend adding a ½" (1.3 cm) margin all around the base size.

2. Using the viewfinder, find the part of the decorative paper you want to use. Trace 2 shapes of the desired size onto the paper and cut.

3. Brush diluted PVA glue on one face of the base and around the edge. Position 1 piece of decorative paper onto the base and press down to affix. (Fig. 1)

4. Working from the center toward the edge, brush diluted PVA glue across the top of the paper, smoothing out any air bubbles as you brush. Brush around the edge as well, to affix the paper all around and wet the margins to soften

them. Later, this makes tearing the margins away easier and more precise. Set aside to dry on the support stand for about 5 minutes. (Fig. 2)

5. Gently tear off the excess paper around the edge, leaving only the face and edge covered. Let dry.

6. Turn over the base, and repeat Steps 3 to 5 on the other side. Brush diluted PVA glue on both faces and around the edge of the base, smoothing it gently with your finger. Let dry.

NOTE This is a great way to make the most of a really nice piece of washi paper handmade paper, or any other thin and flexible paper. You can use it to cover a paper base of any kind.

Embellishing with Decorative Paper Napkins

This technique is a great way of making the most of leftover paper napkins in your cupboard. Paper napkins usually have several layers, but since only the top one is decorated, separate this, and use it on its own for decorating.

MATERIALS

Decorative paper napkin
Paper base to be covered
Diluted PVA glue

TOOLS

Viewfinder (page 30)
Pencil
Scissors
Paintbrush
Support stand

DIRECTIONS

1. Determine the size of napkin you'll need to cover the base. In general, I recommend adding a ½" (1.3 cm) margin all around the base size.

2. Using the viewfinder, find the part of the napkin you want to use. Trace 2 shapes of the desired size onto the napkin and cut.

3. Gently separate the top layer of the cut napkin from the other layers. Set aside the other layers for another use.

4. Position 1 napkin shape onto one face of the base. Working from the center of the base toward the edge, gently brush diluted PVA glue onto the napkin, smoothing out any air bubbles as you brush. Brush around the edge as well, to affix the napkin all around. Set aside to dry on the support stand for about 5 minutes.

Paper napkins are very delicate so don't apply PVA glue to your paper base before placing the napkin. Work gently with your paintbrush when affixing the napkins, and sure you don't apply too much glue, since napkins are thin and can tear easily.

5. Gently tear off the excess napkin around the edge, leaving only the face and edge covered. Let dry.

6. Turn over the base and repeat Steps 4 and 5 on the other side. Brush diluted PVA glue around the edge of the piece, smoothing it very gently with your finger. Let dry.

Decorating with Bits and Pieces

With this technique, you'll assemble scraps of special paper into a beautiful and unique paper collage. It's a terrific way to make the most of leftover paper pieces from other decorating projects, bits of fancy wrapping paper and small pieces of stationary.

MATERIALS

Various multicolored pieces of paper, straight edges torn off

Diluted PVA glue

Paper base to be covered

TOOLS

Paintbrush

Support stand

DIRECTIONS

1. Select the papers for your project and tear them into small pieces. (Fig. 1)

2. Brush diluted PVA glue on one face and around the edge of the base.

3. Brush diluted PVA glue on both sides of a paper piece, and affix to one side of the base.

4. Repeat Step 3 to create a colorful paper carpet on one face of the base. Overlap the pieces and use transparent pieces to create several different hues. Make sure that the edge of the base is covered as well. Brush around the edge to affix the papers all around. Set aside to dry on the support stand for about 5 minutes.

1   2

5. Gently tear off the excess paper around the edge, leaving only the face and edge covered. Let dry. (Fig. 2)

6. Turn over the base and repeat Steps 2 to 5 on the other side. Brush diluted PVA glue around the edge of the base, smoothing it gently with your finger. Let dry.

Decorating Beads with Washi Paper

With this technique, you can create a delicate and distinctive paper covering for plastic or wooden beads. If you like, replace the washi paper with thin handmade paper, a piece of leftover stationary or the top layer of a decorative paper napkin.

MATERIALS

Plastic or wooden bead of your choice
1 sheet of washi paper
Tie wire, 19-gauge (0.9 mm)
Diluted PVA glue

TOOLS

Wire cutters
Paintbrush
Support stand

DIRECTIONS

1. Tear a piece of washi paper that is about ½" (1.3 cm) longer than the bead's perimeter and a bit wider than its diameter.

2. Cut a piece of tie wire that is about 7" (18 cm) longer than the bead. Insert the wire through the hole in the bead, and position the bead in the middle of the wire. Bend the wire on either side of the bead to make a U shape. This wire supports the bead as you proceed.

3. Brush diluted PVA glue over the entire bead. Affix one edge of the washi paper to the bead by pressing it onto the glue. Wrap the washi paper around the bead, using a paintbrush dipped in diluted PVA glue to affix. The texture will likely be a bit wrinkly. Press the surface gently with the paintbrush or your fingertips as you wrap. (Fig. 1)

1

2

4. Let the bead dry for a bit using the support stand, then make adjustments to the surface by pressing and smoothing it with your fingertips. Make sure the washi is firmly attached to the bead.

5. Brush with a bit more diluted PVA glue, if necessary, and smooth out air bubbles. Let dry. (Fig. 2)

Decorating with Metallic Paints

For a sparkling metallic finish, try dabbing some gold or silver paint onto your project. As in previous techniques, the secret is to use a variety of hues and shades.

MATERIALS

Metallic gold, silver and copper paint
Metallic gold, silver and copper dust
PVA glue
Paper base to be decorated
Water

TOOLS

Plastic container
Paintbrush

DIRECTIONS

1. Put a small quantity of each paint color in a container. Sprinkle some metallic dust into the container as well, and mix it with a bit of PVA glue. Mix the dust into some of the paints in the container but leave some of the paints without dust in order to allow for a variety of options.

2. Dip the paintbrush into the dust mixture and the paints, mixing them with a bit of water to dilute, if necessary.

3. Tap the mixture onto the paper base, integrating different shades and colors until you are pleased with the results.

NOTE You may want to add a bit of acrylic paint to the mixture as well, to give it a special hue (see the Golden Galaxy Necklace, pages 66–69).

Decorating with Acrylic Paints

Bristol or cardboard bases that have been covered with paper pieces make excellent tiny canvases for painting. I find acrylic paints best for painting on paper, since the paper absorbs the paint beautifully.

Undiluted acrylic paints create an opaque finish. Acrylic paint diluted with water dries as a transparent coating that is lighter than the original color. The more you dilute the paint, the more transparent the coating.

I suggest experimenting with a variety colors before painting a paper base. Use a plastic container as a palette and dab a bit of each color on it. Dip a paintbrush in water and dilute some of the dabs of color, leaving others as they are. You can also combine some of the colors.

When you're ready to paint, dip a paintbrush in the desired color and tap it on your project piece. Don't be afraid to mix colors together and tap them on any way you wish. You can also lighten shades with white paint or thin the paint with water, creating a rainbow of hues on the paper base. I'm sure you'll be delighted at the artistic results you achieve.

Decorating with Gold Dust Mixture

Adding gold dust to a handmade decorated paper piece gives it a touch of elegance. Follow the simple instructions below to make a gold dust mixture that has just the right amount of sparkle. This mixture can be stored for several weeks in a tightly sealed container.

MATERIALS

PVA glue

Water

Gold dust

Silver dust

Absorbent cotton fabric

Paper base to be decorated

TOOLS

Small bowl

Paintbrush

Support stand

Sealable container

DIRECTIONS

1. Place 1 teaspoon of PVA glue into a small bowl and mix with 6 teaspoons of water. Add a dash of gold dust, allowing it form a flat "cloud" of about 1 x 2⅓" (2 x 6 cm) in the center of the dish. If you'd like a more metallic effect, dip a dry paintbrush in silver dust and mix it into the mixture.

TIP The secret of creating just the right metallic effect is to experiment with the quantity of gold and silver dust in the mixture. Trust your instincts.

1

2. Mix thoroughly with the paintbrush until the mixture becomes smooth and almost transparent. Wash the paintbrush to remove any extra dust and dab with a piece of cotton fabric to absorb excess water before using the mixture to decorate the paper base.

3. Trickle drops of the mixture onto the paper base. Allow the mixture to flow and penetrate through wrinkles in the surface of the piece. This will result in an attractive metallic look. (Fig. 1)

4. Use cotton fabric to absorb excess mixture, or trickle on more mixture. When the desired effect has been achieved, set the piece aside on the support stand to dry.

Jewelry-making Techniques

The variety of jewelry-making techniques recommended in the project instructions are described below.

Flattening crimp beads

Crimp beads are used to hold beads, chains and wires in place. They come in various sizes and styles and should be selected to suit the diameter of the object they will hold.

1. Slide the crimp bead along the chain or wire until it reaches the desired location.

2. Grasp the crimp bead with flat-nose pliers, positioning the pliers so that the flattened crimp bead is oriented in the desired direction.

3. Gently press the crimp bead with the pliers, flattening it and securing it into place.

Opening and closing jump rings or loops

You'll need to open jump rings, links and other types of loops in most jewelry-making projects. I recommend doing this with 2 sets of pliers, in the following manner.

1. Grip one side of the jump ring with pliers, as close to the opening as possible.

2. With the other set of pliers, grip the jump ring on the other side of the opening. Move one set of pliers towards you and the other set away from you to create a space that is large enough for stringing the desired object.

3. When you are finished stringing objects onto the open jump ring, close the space by drawing the pliers in the reverse direction.

1   2

Making dangling chains

This simple technique can be used to make dangling chains of any length. If you want the lengths to be even, fold the chain in half in Step 1. If you want different lengths, fold the chain as desired in Step 1.

1. Fold the chain in half (or as desired) and slide the ends into a crimp bead. (Fig. 1)

2. Draw the crimp bead up toward the folded end of the chain, forming a small loop at that end.

3. Grasp the crimp bead with flat-nose pliers and flatten to secure. (Fig. 2)

Forming loops in wire, eye pins or head pins

To secure beads and other objects onto wires, head pins and eye pins, you'll often have to make a loop in the wire. It may take a bit of practice to make a loop that is smooth and attractive, so be patient. As a general rule, leave yourself about ⅓" (9 mm) to make the loop.

1. Using a pair of round-nose pliers, bend the wire at a 90-degree angle away from you.

2. Grasp the bent wire with the pliers just beyond the bend, and pull the tip of the wire back towards you.

3. Using the tip of the pliers, draw the wire all the way around, making a loop at the tip.

4. If you plan to string something onto the loop, don't close it completely. Otherwise, draw the wire all the way around to close the loop.

Making dangling beads

Dangling beads add a dynamic, often musical aspect to jewelry. I generally use head pins or eye pins that are ¾" (2 cm) long for stringing a single bead. If you want to string two or more beads, use longer head pins or eye pins, or a piece of brass wire. Adjust the length of the stringing material you select according to the number of beads you plan to string.

1. String the bead onto the head pin. Draw the bead down to the base of the head pin.

2. Allow ⅓" (9 mm) to extend above the bead, and then trim the excess wire. Form a loop at the tip with round-nose pliers.

JEWELRY DESIGNS

Glamorous Hoop Pendant

In order to make this design, you'll need to wrap both the outer and inner edge of the paper piece with strips of computer paper. The piece is striking, both in size and design, and just right for displaying on its own, without any beads, crystals, or other embellishments. As for the chain, it's actually a large-link gold belt.

MATERIALS

Hoop Pendant

Corrugated Paper Base (page 22), hoop shape, 4" (10 cm) outside diameter; 1¾" (4.5 cm) inside diameter

Diluted PVA glue

1 sheet of washi paper, 9 x 12" (21 x 30 cm)

Gloss glaze

Necklace

Gold-plated large link chain, about 30" (76 cm) long

1 large gold-plated clasp

TOOLS

Viewfinder (page 30)

Pencil

Compass

Utility knife

Paintbrushes

Flat-nose pliers

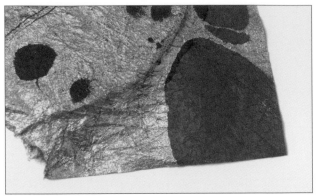

1

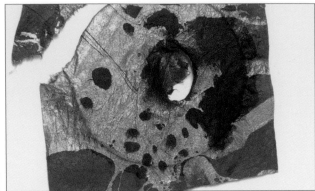

2

DIRECTIONS

Hoop Pendant

1. Using the viewfinder, find 2 areas of the washi paper that you want to use for the top layer. Trace the hoop-shaped corrugated cardboard base, adding a margin of about ½" (1.3 cm) around the outer and inner edges. Cut the shapes.

2. Brush diluted PVA glue on one face of the base and along the outside and inside edges. Position 1 piece of washi paper on top and affix. (Fig. 1)

3. Working from the center of the hoop toward the edge, brush diluted PVA glue across the top of the paper, smoothing out any air bubbles as you brush. Brush around the outside and inside edges as well, pressing gently with the paintbrush to soften the paper and affix it all around. Set aside to dry for about 5 minutes.

4. Gently tear off the excess paper all around, leaving only the face and outside edges covered. Gently press the paper along

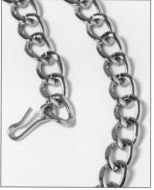

3　　　　　　　　4

the inner edge of the hoop and tear off the excess paper here. Brush the inside edge with diluted PVA glue to form an even and smooth surface. Let dry. (Fig. 2)

5. Repeat Steps 2 to 4 on the other face of the hoop.

6. Brush gloss glaze on both faces and let dry.

Necklace

7. Insert one end of the chain through the hole of the Hoop Pendant, from front to back. Wrap the chain once around the pendant, then draw it through the hole again, from front to back. (Fig. 3)

8. Connect the clasp to one end of the chain. (Fig. 4)

Sunset Shell Necklace

The sun may have already set, but with this necklace around your neck, the luminous colors of sunset will stay with you all evening. As with all necklace designs, adjust the length of the ribbon to your own preference.

MATERIALS

Shell Pendant

1 Concave Paper Shell (page 26), about 1½" (4 cm) long

Red, yellow and orange acrylic paints

Water

Gold glitter glue

Gloss glaze

1 brass wire, 24-gauge (0.5 mm), 4" (10 cm) long

2 multifaceted violet glass beads, ⅛" (3 mm) diameter

2 multifaceted bright pink glass beads, ¼" (6 mm) diameter

2 gold-plated decorative bead caps, ⅓" (9 mm) diameter

1 fuchsia glass bead, ½" (1.3 cm) diameter

Delicate gold-plated chain, 6⅓" (16 cm) long

1 gold-plated jump ring, 4 mm

Neck Ribbon

Orange organdy ribbon, 1" (2.5 cm) wide, about 20" (51 cm) long

Gold thread

2 gold-plated tube beads, ⅛" (4 mm) inside diameter, ¼" (6 mm) overall diameter

1 gold-plated hoop, ¼" (6 mm) diameter

2 gold-plated cord tips with connecting rings

1 gold-plated clasp

2 gold-plated jump rings, ³⁄₁₆" (5 mm)

TOOLS

Plastic container for mixing paint

Paintbrushes

Support stand

Needle

Scissors

Flat-nose pliers

Wire cutter

Round-nose pliers

1   2   3   4

DIRECTIONS

Shell Pendant

1. Mix some red and yellow paint in a container until you have a few shades of orange, or use prepared orange paint and make various shades by adding red or yellow paint. Dilute some of the paint with water for a variety of consistencies (page 39).

2. Using a paintbrush, lightly tap paint on spots of the Concave Paper Shell, alternating with different shades of orange, until you like the result. (Fig. 1)

3. Mix a bit of red paint into the orange paint to get a darker shade of orange, and use this to paint the edge of the shell. Let dry. (Fig. 2)

4. Turn over the shell and repeat Step 2 to paint the back. Let dry.

5. Place some glitter glue on the front of the shell and spread it gently with your finger. Let dry, then repeat on the back of the piece. Let dry.

6. Brush gloss glaze on both sides of the piece and let dry.

7. Using the needle, pierce a hole in the lower middle of the shell, about 1/6" (4 mm) from the bottom. Pierce another hole in the upper middle of the shell, about 1/6" (4 mm) from the top rim.

8. Make a loop at the tip of the brass wire. Insert the straight end of the wire upward through the hole at the bottom of the shell. String on 1 violet bead, 1 bright pink bead, 1 bead cap, 1 fuchsia bead, 1 bead cap, 1 bright pink bead and 1 violet bead. Insert the wire through the hole at the top of the shell. (Fig. 3)

9. Allow 1/3" (9 mm) of wire to extend above the top of the shell. Trim the excess wire and make a loop at the tip that is oriented parallel to the top of the shell. Do not close the loop. (Fig. 4)

10. Cut the chain into 4 equal pieces, each measuring about

5　　　　　　　　6　　　　　　　　7　　　　　　　　8

1½" (4 cm). Open the jump ring and slide it through the last link of all 4 chains. Slide the jump ring through the loop at the bottom of the shell and close the jump ring. (Fig. 5)

Neck Ribbon

11. Make two ½" (1.3 cm) folds at one end of the ribbon. (Fig. 6)

12. Fold the folded section in half, by folding one side toward the center of the ribbon and then folding the other side toward the center, overlapping the first side. Sew together to secure the fold. (Fig. 7)

13. Roll the tip of the unfinished end of ribbon until it is narrow enough for sliding on beads. Slide on 1 gold-plated tube bead, drawing it along until it is about 5" (13 cm) from the sewed end. Slide the gold-plated hoop onto the ribbon, drawing it along until it is about 2¾" (7 cm) from the tube bead. Slide the other gold-plated tube bead onto the ribbon, and position it about 2¾" (7 cm) from the hoop. The hoop

should now be at the center of the ribbon, and the tube beads should be positioned at an equal distance from the center.

14. Double check the length of the necklace and trim excess ribbon if necessary. Repeat Steps 11 and 12 to fold and sew the other end of the ribbon.

15. Slide each ribbon end into a cord tip, and flatten with the flat-nose pliers. Open 2 jump rings and slide each one into a ring on a cord tip. Slide half the clasp onto each jump ring. Close the jump rings. (Fig. 8)

16. Slide the top loop of the shell pendant onto the hoop at the middle of the ribbon; then close the loop.

Oval Bead
Opera Necklace

♕

This asymmetrical yet balanced necklace can be worn as a single or double strand. Depending on how it hangs, the necklace will look a little bit different every time. This unique design deserves a really special clasp that can be positioned at the collarbone for maximum effect.

MATERIALS

Sculpted Oval Beads

7 Paper Pulp Beads (page 24), tie wire still inside, oval, ranging in size from 1 x 1⅓" (2.5 x 3.5 cm) to 1⅓ x 2" (3.5 x 5 cm)

Several sheets of washi paper, black with gold design, 9 x 12" (21 x 30 cm)

Diluted PVA glue

Varnish (matte recommended)

Necklace

Brass wire, 24-gauge (0.5 mm)

Elegant gold-plated chain, medium links, 29" (74 cm) long

1 gold-plated clasp

TOOLS

Viewfinder (page 30)

Pencil

Paintbrushes

Ruler

Wire cutters

Round-nose pliers

Flat-nose pliers

1

2

DIRECTIONS

Sculpted Oval Beads

1. Using the viewfinder, find 2 parts of the washi paper you want to use for the top layer of 1 bead. Trace the outline of 1 paper pulp bead onto the back of the washi paper, adding a ¼" (6 mm) margin all around. Cut or tear the paper.

2. Trace the torn piece onto another area of the washi paper and cut or tear to make another similar shape.

3. Brush diluted PVA glue on one side of the bead, and position one of the pieces of washi paper on this side of the bead. Working from the center of the bead toward the edge, brush diluted PVA glue across the top of the washi paper, smoothing out any air bubbles as you brush. Cover the edge of the bead as well. Let dry. (Fig. 1)

4. Repeat Step 3 on the other side of the bead with the other piece of washi paper. Let dry.

5. Repeat Steps 1 to 4 with the 6 other beads. Brush varnish on the beads and let dry. Carefully remove the tie wire from each bead.

Necklace

6. Cut a piece of brass wire that is about 1" (2.5 cm) longer than the sculpted oval bead you want to string. Make a loop at one end of the wire, but don't close the loop. Insert the straight end of the wire through the tunnel of one bead. Allow ⅓" (9 mm) of wire to extend above the bead, and trim the excess wire. Make a loop at this end of the wire, but don't close.

7. Repeat Step 6 with the other 6 beads, adjusting the size of the wire you cut to the size of the bead you are stringing.

3

8. Cut the chain (or open the links) into 8 pieces, with the following measurements: four 2½" (6.4 cm) pieces; one 1½" (4 cm) piece; one 11" (28 cm) piece; two 3¼" (8 cm) pieces.

9. Place the beads and chain pieces on your work surface and arrange as desired. I suggest positioning the 11" (28 cm) chain at the back of the necklace, so that the necklace sits comfortably when worn. Also, note that in this design, the clasp is meant to be visible when worn, so there's no need to situate it at the back of the necklace.

10. When you're satisfied with the arrangement, connect 1 piece of chain to each half of the clasp. (Fig. 2)

11. Connect the rest of the chains to the beads by stringing the end links on each chain into the open loops on the beads. Close the loops. (Fig. 3)

For variety, use different decorative papers and several chain types.

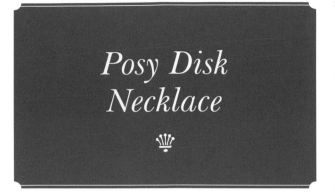

Posy Disk Necklace

Seven large disks of various sizes connected by seven pieces of chain of various lengths—add up to a magnificent design. Each disk is covered with a bright floral pattern, giving the necklace a vivacious personality.

MATERIALS

Posy Disks

7 Corrugated Cardboard Bases (page 22), tie wire still inside, round, in the following measurements:
3 disks of 3" (7.6 cm) diameter
2 disks of 2¼" (5.7 cm) diameter
2 disks of 2" (5 cm) diameter

Several identical decorative paper napkins

Diluted PVA glue

Varnish

Necklace

Brass wire, 24-gauge (0.5 mm), about 25" (64 cm) long

Gold-plated link chain, 41" (104 cm) long

TOOLS

Viewfinder (page 30)

Pencil

Scissors

Paintbrushes

Support stand

Ruler

Wire cutters

Flat-nose pliers

Round-nose pliers

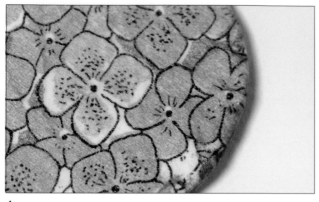

1

2

DIRECTIONS

Posy Disks

1. Using the viewfinder, find 2 parts of the decorative napkin you want to use for the top layer for 1 bead. Trace the outline of 1 Corrugated Cardboard Base onto the back of the decorative napkin, adding a ½" (1.3 cm) margin all around.

2. Cut or tear the napkins rounds and gently separate the top layer from the other layers. Set aside the other layers for another use.

3. Position 1 napkin round on one side of the corresponding base. Working from the center of the base outward, gently brush diluted PVA glue on the surface of the napkin, smoothing out any air bubbles as you brush. Brush around the edge as well to affix the napkin all around. Set aside to dry for about 5 minutes.

4. Gently tear off the excess napkin around the edge, leaving only the face and edge covered. Let dry.

5. Repeat Steps 3 to 4 on the other side of this base. (Fig. 1)

6. Repeat Steps 1 to 5 with the other napkins and bases. Remember to brush diluted PVA glue around the edge of each piece until it is smooth. Let dry.

7. Brush varnish all over each piece and let dry. Carefully remove the tie wires.

Necklace

8. Cut a 4" (10 cm) piece of brass wire and make a loop at one end. Don't close the loop. Insert the straight end of the wire through the tunnel of one 3" (7.6 cm) Posy Disk. Allow ⅓" (9 mm) wire to extend above the top of the disk, and trim the excess wire. Make a loop at this end of the wire, but don't close.

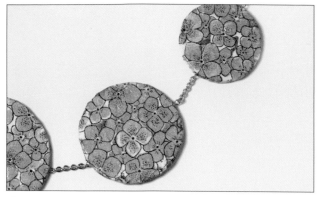

3

9. Repeat Step 8 with the other 6 Posy Disks, adjusting the size of the wire you cut to the size of the disk you are stringing.

10. Cut the chain (or open the links) into 7 pieces, with the following measurements: four ¾" (2 cm) pieces; one 2½" (6.4 cm) piece; one 14" (35 cm) piece; one 22" (55 cm) piece.

11. Place the Posy Disks and chain pieces on your work surface and arrange as desired. I suggest positioning the 22" (55 cm) chain at the back of the necklace, and the 14" (35 cm) chain at the front of the short necklace, so that the necklace sits comfortably when worn.

12. When you're satisfied with the arrangement, connect the chains to the disks by stringing the end links on each chain piece into the open loops on the Posy Disks. Close the loops. (Figs. 2 and 3)

In the design, the paper base is covered in orange paper and then with a decorative napkin.

Vanity Flair Necklace

❦

Ribbons, paper flowers, trinkets and charms combine to create a carefree and pretty accessory. You'll find the ribbon and plastic flowers at most craft shops.

MATERIALS

Flower Stacks

1 sheet of thick handmade paper, metallic blue, 9 x 12" (21 x 30 cm)

1 sheet of thick handmade paper, metallic gold, 9 x 12" (21 x 30 cm)

Washi paper, white with gold thread, 9 x 12" (21 x 30 cm)

Plastic wrap

Transparent fabric hardener

3 multifaceted flat plastic bead flowers, ¾" (2 cm) diameter,

3 gold-plated decorative beads, ³/₁₆" (5 mm) diameter

Nickel silver wire, 24-gauge (0.5 mm), 8" (20 cm) long

Neck Ribbon

14 blue multifaceted glass beads, ¼" (6 mm) diameter

20 gold-plated head pins, ¾" (2 cm) long

6 white pearl beads, ⅛" (3 mm) diameter

2 gold-plated jump rings, ³/₁₆" (5 mm)

2 gold-plated curved tube beads with loops, 1" (2.5 cm) long

Blue organdy ribbon, 1" (2.5 cm) wide, 30" (76 cm) long

TOOLS

Pencil

Compass

Scissors

Paintbrushes

Thick needle

Round-nose pliers

Wire cutters

Metalwork file

Flat-nose pliers

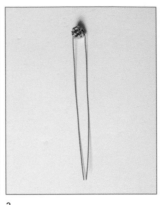

1   2   3   4

DIRECTIONS

Flower Stacks

1. Trace Drawing 1 (page 126), copy 3 times onto blue handmade paper and cut. (Fig. 1)

2. Draw 6 circles, each with a 1½" (4 cm) diameter, on the gold handmade paper and cut.

3. Trace Drawing 2 (page 126), copy 3 times onto the white washi paper and cut. (Fig. 2)

4. Cut slits in the white rounds, as shown in the drawing, to make "leaves." Fold the leaves to give them a sense of motion.

5. Spread plastic wrap on your work area and arrange the blue flowers and gold rounds on top, all upside down.

Brush fabric hardener on the back of each shape and let dry for about 1 hour.

6. Arrange the white rounds on the plastic wrap and brush one side with fabric hardener. Let dry for about 15 minutes. Turn the white rounds over and brush fabric hardener on the other side as well. Let dry for about 1 hour.

7. Press your thumb in the center of each blue paper flower to form a depression.

8. Mark the center of each paper cutting and plastic flower, and pierce a hole in each with the needle.

9. Form 3 identical stacks, each consisting of the following: 1 gold circle (upside down); 1 white circle with leaves; 1 gold circle; 1 blue paper flower; 1 plastic flower.

10. Cut a 4" (10 cm) piece of nickel silver wire. Slide a gold bead onto the wire and draw it along until it reaches the middle of the wire. Fold the wire in half. (Fig. 3)

5

6

7

11. Holding both ends of the wire together, insert the ends into the holes in the stack, starting with the plastic flower at top and drawing the wire through all the elements until you reach the gold circle at the bottom. Pull the wire until the gold bead sits securely on top of the plastic flower.

12. Spread the two wires apart and allow 1" (2.5 cm) to extend from each end. Cut the excess wire and file the tips with the metalwork file. Grip a wire tip with the round-nose pliers and form a coil with 2 or 3 loops. Repeat with the other wire tip. (Fig. 4) Press the two coils together to form 1 coil of about ⅕" (5 mm).

13. Repeat Steps 10 to 12 to make 2 more Flower Stacks. (Fig. 5)

Neck Ribbon

14. String 1 blue glass bead onto a head pin. Allow ⅓" (9 mm) of wire to extend above the bead and trim the excess wire. Make a loop at the tip.

15. Repeat Step 14 another 5 times to make a total of 6 dangling blue beads.

16. String 1 pearl bead and 1 blue glass bead onto a head pin. Allow ⅓" (9 mm) of wire to extend above the bead, and trim the excess wire. Make a loop at the tip.

17. Repeat Step 16 another 5 times to make a total of 6 dangling pearl and blue beads.

18. Open a jump ring and string on 3 dangling blue beads and 3 dangling pearl and blue beads, alternating them. (Fig. 6)

19. Insert the jump ring through the loop on a tube bead and close. (Fig. 7)

8   9

20. Repeat Steps 18 and 19 with the other dangling beads and tube bead.

21. Roll the tip at one end of the ribbon and insert it through the coil under 1 Flower Stack. Slide the Flower Stack along until it reaches the middle of the ribbon. (Fig. 8)

22. String 1 decorated tube bead onto one end of the ribbon, sliding it along until it is about ¼" (6 mm) from the Flower Stack. Insert this end of the ribbon into the coil under the second Flower Stack and slide the Flower Stack until it is about ⅔" (1.7 cm) from the tube bead. (Fig. 9)

23. Repeat Step 22 at the other end of the ribbon, with the other decorated tube bead and Flower Stack.

24. Brush fabric hardener on the tips of the ribbon. Let dry.

Golden Galaxy Necklace

✿

This dazzling necklace features glorious handmade beads, colorful plastic beads and a decorative gold chain. Select a chain with interesting links to maximize the impact of the design.

MATERIALS

Sparkling Paper Beads

5 Sculpted Paper Beads (page 28), tie wire still inside, elongated shapes, in the following dimensions:
3 star shapes, 1½" (4 cm) long
2 diamond shapes, 1½" (4 cm) long

Red, blue, purple and metallic acrylic paints

Water

Gold Dust Mixture (page 40)

Varnish

5 gold-plated eye pins, 2½" (6.4 cm) long

Necklace

18 floral gold-plated bead caps, ⅓" (9 mm) diameter

9 multicolored glittery plastic beads, ⅓" (9 mm) diameter

9 gold-plated eye pins, 1" (2.5 cm) long

28 gold-plated jump rings, ¼" (6 mm)

Medium-link gold-plated chain, about 37" (94 cm) long

TOOLS

Paintbrushes

Plastic container for mixing paint

Support stand

Wire cutters

Round-nose pliers

Flat-nose pliers

1   2   3   4

DIRECTIONS

Sparkling Paper Beads

1. Place a bit of each paint color in a plastic container. Mix some of the paints together for a variety of shades. Dilute some of the paint with water for a variety of consistencies (page 39).

2. Tap each Sculpted Paper Bead with a different color of paint, as follows: 1 star shape with red; 2 star shapes with blue and gold dust mixture; 2 diamond shapes with purple and metallic color. Let dry.

3. Tap some gold dust mixture on the red and blue beads. Let dry. Brush varnish on the beads and let dry.

4. Carefully remove the tie wire from each bead and insert a gold-plated eye pin through the resulting tunnel. Allow ⅓" (9 mm) of wire to extend above the top of each bead (Fig. 1). Trim the excess wire and make a loop at the tip.

Necklace

5. String 1 gold-plated bead cap, 1 plastic bead and 1 gold-plated bead cap onto a gold-plated eye pin. Allow ⅓" (9 mm) of wire to extend above the bead cap. Trim the excess wire and make a loop at the tip. (Fig. 2)

6. Repeat Step 5 to string the rest of the bead caps and plastic beads onto eye pins.

7. Open the jump rings and insert 1 jump ring through the loops at either end of each dangling bead and each Sparkling Paper Bead. Don't close the jump rings.

8. Cut the chain (or open the links) into 11 pieces, with the following measurements: two 9½" (24 cm) pieces; four 2¼" (5.7 cm) pieces; three 1¾" (4.5 cm) pieces; one 2¾" (7 cm) piece; one 1¼" (3 cm) piece.

9. Arrange the beads and chain pieces on your work surface. I suggest positioning one 9½" (24 cm) chain at the back of the necklace and the other 9½" (24 cm) chain at the front of the short necklace, so that the necklace sits comfortably on the neck. As for the other chains and beads, arrange as desired. Notice that while most of the beads are connected to chains on either side, some of the beads are connected to other beads. If you connect beads together, remove any extra jump rings. (Figs. 3 and 4)

10. When you're satisfied with the arrangement, connect the chains and beads using the jump rings on either side of each eye pin. Close all the jump rings.

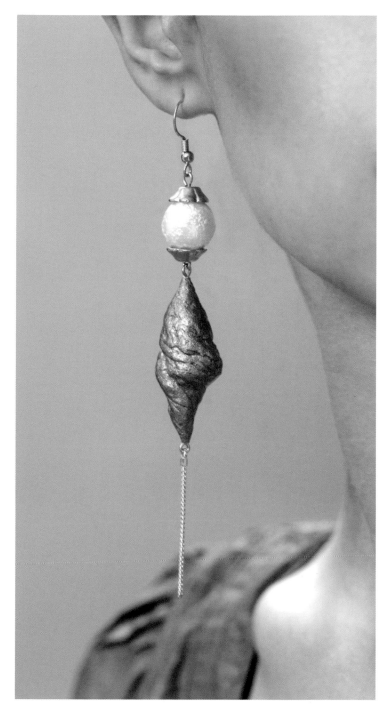

Combine elongated paper beads with round pearl beads for a set of dangling earrings.

Ebony and Gold Necklace

This lustrous and dramatic necklace radiates beauty and elegance. As with all necklace designs, adjust the length of the ribbon to your own preference.

MATERIALS

Ebony and Gold Pendant

1 Bristol Board Base (page 20), tie wire still inside, round, about 2½" (6.4 cm) diameter

1 sheet of washi paper, black with gold design, 9 x 12" (21 x 30 cm)

Diluted PVA glue

Varnish

Delicate gold-plated rope chain, 3¼" (8 cm) long

1 gold-plated crimp bead

Brass wire, 24-gauge (0.5 mm), 4" (10 cm) long

1 gold-plated bead, ⅛" (4 mm) diameter

1 black fabric bead, ⅜" (1 cm) diameter

1 gold-plated bead, ¼" (6 mm) diameter

1 gold-plated bead, ½" (1.3 cm) diameter

Neck Ribbon

Green organdy ribbon, 1" (2.5 cm) wide, about 20" (50 cm) long

Gold organdy ribbon with stiff edges, 1½" (4 cm) wide, about 20" (50 cm) long

Gold thread

3 gold-plated flat tube beads, ¼" (6 mm) inside diameter, ⅓" (9 mm) outside diameter, ½" (1.3 cm) long

2 cord tips with connecting rings

3 gold-plated jump rings: two ⅕" (5 mm) jump rings and one ⅛" (3 mm) jump ring

1 gold-plated clasp

Delicate gold-plated chain, 1½" (4 cm) long

TOOLS

Viewfinder (page 30)	Flat-nose pliers
Pencil	Round-nose pliers
Scissors	Wire cutters
Paintbrush	Needle
Support stand	

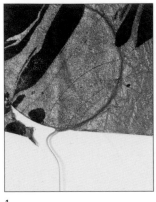

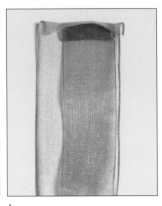

1   2   3   4

DIRECTIONS

Ebony and Gold Pendant

1. Using the viewfinder, find the part of the washi paper you want to use to cover the base. Draw 2 circles on the back, each 3½" (9 cm) in diameter, and cut or tear the paper. (Fig. 1)

2. Brush diluted PVA glue on one face of the Bristol Board Base and around the edges. Position the washi paper on the base and affix.

3. Brush diluted PVA glue on the surface of the washi paper, working from the center outward and smoothing out air bubbles as you brush. Brush around the edges as well. Let dry for about 5 minutes.

4. Gently tear off excess paper, leaving only the face and edges covered. Let dry.

5. Repeat Steps 2 to 4 on the other side of the base, brushing around the edges with diluted glue until smooth. Let dry. Brush varnish on both faces of the base and let dry.

6. Fold the rope chain in half and slide both ends into a crimp bead. Draw the crimp bead up toward the folded end of the chain, creating a small loop at that end. Flatten the crimp bead with the flat-nose pliers. (Fig 2)

7. Make a loop at one end of the brass wire. Do not close the loop. String the loop in the chain onto this loop; then close the loop in the brass wire.

8. Insert the straight end of the wire into the ⅛" (4 mm) gold-plated bead, the black fabric bead, and the ¼" (6 mm) gold-plated bead.

9. Carefully remove the tie wire from the paper piece. String it onto the brass wire, then string on the ½" (1.3 cm) gold-plated bead. Allow ⅓" (9 mm) of wire to extend above the top of the bead, then trim the excess wire and make a loop at the tip. (Fig. 3)

5   6   7   8

Neck Ribbon

10. Make two ¼" (6 mm) folds at one end of the green ribbon. Lay the green ribbon flatly on the top center of the gold ribbon, with the folded end about ¼" (6 mm) from the tip. Fold the tip of the gold ribbon over the folded end of the green ribbon. (Fig. 4)

11. Fold one side of the folded section toward the center of the ribbon. Fold the other side toward the center, overlapping the first side. Sew the ends together to secure the folds. (Fig 5)

12. Slide this end of the ribbon into a cord tip. Make sure the ribbon is securely tucked inside, then flatten with the flat-nose pliers.

13. Roll the tip of the unfinished end of ribbon until it is narrow enough for sliding on the beads, then gently slide on 3 gold-plated tube beads: position 1 bead about 4" (10 cm) from the sewn end, 1 bead at the center of the necklace and 1 bead about 4" (10 cm) from the unfinished end. (Fig. 6)

14. Repeat Steps 10 to 12 at the other end of the ribbon. (Fig. 7)

15. Open the two ⅕" (5 mm) jump rings and insert one into each cord tip. Slide one part of the clasp onto each jump ring, then close the jump rings.

16. Slide the gold-plated chain through the center bead of the necklace. Open the ⅛" (3 mm) jump ring and slide it onto the first and last links of the chain.

17. Slide the loop at the top of the Ebony and Gold Pendant onto the jump ring, then close the jump ring. (Fig. 8)

Fiery Flower Pendant

This necklace combines a striking pendant with an unusual bead. The dangling chain, strung on a leather cord, magnifies the brightness of the fiery flower. Adjust the length of the cord according to your preference.

MATERIALS

Flower Pendant

Decorative paper napkin

Corrugated Cardboard Base (page 22), tie wire still inside, round, 2½" (6.4 cm) diameter

Diluted PVA glue

Gloss glaze

Brass wire, 24-gauge (0.5 mm), about 8" (20 cm) long

Delicate gold-plated rope chain, 3¼" (8 cm) long

1 decorative wooden bead, 1¼" (3 cm) diameter

1 silver crimp bead

Necklace

Brown leather cord, ⅛" (3 mm) diameter, 19" (47 cm) long

3 brass jump rings, ¼" (6 mm)

2 brass cord tips with connecting rings

1 brass clasp

TOOLS

Viewfinder (page 30)

Pencil

Scissors

Support stand

Paintbrush

Round-nose pliers

Ruler

Wire cutters

Flat-nose pliers

1   2   3   4

DIRECTIONS

4. Gently tear off the excess napkin, leaving only the face and edge covered. Let dry.

5. Repeat Steps 3 and 4 on the other side of the base, brushing around the edge for a final smoothing. Let dry. Brush gloss glaze on both sides of the piece and let dry.

6. Cut a 3½" (9 cm) piece of brass wire and make a loop at one end.

Flower Pendant

1. Using the viewfinder, find the part of the napkin you want to use to cover the base. Draw 2 circles, each with a 3" (7.6 cm) diameter, on the decorative napkin and cut. (Fig. 1)

2. Gently separate the top layer of the napkin rounds from the other layers. Reserve the bottom layers for another use.

3. Position one napkin round on one face of a Corrugated Cardboard Base. Gently brush diluted PVA glue on the surface of the napkin, working from the center of the pendant toward the edges. Smooth out air bubbles as you brush and press gently at the edges to soften the napkin. Let dry for about 5 minutes. (Fig. 2)

7. Remove the tie wire from the base and insert the straight end of the brass wire through the resulting tunnel. Allow ⅓" (9 mm) of the wire to extend from the top of the base and trim the excess wire. Make a loop at the tip of the wire but do not close the loop.

8. Draw the chain through the loop at the bottom of the pendant. Insert both ends of the chain through the crimp bead. Draw the crimp bead up toward the folded end of the chain, creating a small loop at that end. Flatten the crimp bead with flat-nose pliers. (Fig. 3)

5   6

9. Cut a 3" (7.6 cm) piece of brass wire and make a double loop at one end.

10. Insert the straight end of the wire through the wooden bead. Allow ⅔" (1.7 cm) of wire to extend above the top, and trim the excess wire. Make a double loop at the tip of the wire.

11. String the loop below the bead onto the open loop at the top of the pendant. Close the loop. (Fig. 4)

Necklace

12. Slide 1 jump ring onto the leather cord and string it on the loop at the top of the wooden bead. Close the loop. (Fig. 5)

13. Slide each end of the leather cord into a cord tip, and flatten the tips with the flat-nose pliers.

14. Open 2 jump rings, slide each one onto a cord tip and slide one of the clasp parts onto each jump ring. Close the jump rings. (Fig. 6)

This dramatic option features a large round pendant, sparkling bead and dangling chain.

I wanted a really delicate pendant for this design, so I used thin corrugated board for the base and covered it with just 1 layer of computer paper. Thanks to the fine batik paper, gold thread and sparkling glitter, this necklace shimmers with elegance.

MATERIALS

Lime Drop Pendant

Corrugated Board Base (page 22), tie wire still inside, oval, 1¼ x 2¼" (3.2 x 5.7 cm)

Diluted PVA glue

1 sheet of batik paper, multihued yellow and green, 9 x 12" (21 x 30 cm)

Gold thread

PVA glue

Gold glitter glue

Varnish

1 gold-plated crimp bead

Gold-plated rope chain, 3¼" (8 cm) long

Brass wire, 24-gauge (0.5 mm), 4" (10 cm) long

2 gold-plated filigree bead caps, ¼" (6 mm) diameter

Necklace

Elastic gold cord, about 24" (60 cm) long

9 multicolored glittery plastic beads, ⅓" (9 mm) diameter

2 gold-plated cord tips with connecting rings

3 gold-plated jump rings: two ⅕" (5 mm) jump rings and one ⅓" (9 mm) jump ring

1 gold-plated crimp bead

1 gold-plated clasp

TOOLS

Paintbrush

Ruler

Scissors

Pencil

Wire cutters

Flat-nose pliers

Round-nose pliers

Support stand

Viewfinder (page 30)

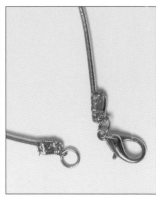

1

2

3

4

DIRECTIONS

Lime Drop Pendant

1. Using the viewfinder, find the part of the batik paper you want to use to cover the base. Trace the Corrugated Board Base onto the paper twice, adding a ½" (1.3 cm) margin all around, and cut.

2. Brush diluted PVA glue on one face and around the edge of the Corrugated Paper Base. Position 1 piece of batik paper on the base and affix.

3. Brush diluted PVA glue on the surface of the paper, working from the center of the base outward and smoothing out air bubbles as you brush. Brush around the edges as well. Let dry for about 5 minutes.

4. Gently tear off excess paper, leaving only the face and edges covered. Let dry.

5. Repeat Steps 2 to 4 on the other side of the base, brushing around the edges with diluted glue until smooth. Let dry.

6. Cut a 32" (80 cm) piece of gold thread. Measure 2" (5 cm) from one end of the thread and place this part of the thread onto the bottom of the oval piece. Apply a drop of PVA glue to that point on the thread and press with your finger to affix. Leave both ends of the thread dangling, and set aside until the glue dries.

7. Carefully draw the longer end of the thread diagonally upward across the face of the base, holding the starting point with your fingers. Wrap the thread over to the back of the base and draw it diagonally downward toward the front.

8. Continue wrapping the thread around the base diagonally several times. (Fig. 1)

9. When you're satisfied with the design, tie both ends of the thread together and brush a little PVA glue on the knot. Delicately apply dots of glue at several more spots along the thread until it is securely affixed to the base. Let dry.

10. Apply some glitter glue, and gently spread it all over the front and back of the base using your fingers. Let dry. Brush varnish all over the base and let dry. Remove the tie wire. (Fig. 2)

11. Fold the rope chain in half and slide both ends into a crimp bead. Draw the crimp bead up toward the folded end of the chain, creating a small loop at that end. Flatten the crimp bead with the flat-nose pliers.

12. Make a small loop at one end of the brass wire, but don't close the loop. Slide the loop of the gold-plated chain through the loop in the wire, then close the loop.

13. Insert the straight end of the brass wire through the tunnel of the pendant. Slide on 1 gold-plated bead cap, 1 multicolored plastic bead and 1 gold-plated bead cap.

14. Allow ⅓" (9 mm) of wire to extend above the bead cap; then trim the excess wire. Make a loop at the top of the wire.

Necklace

15. Measure 4" (10 cm) from one end of the gold cord and tie a knot. Slide a multicolored plastic bead onto the cord and draw it up to the knot. Tie a knot on the other side of the bead. Make sure it is flush against the bead. (Fig. 3)

16. Measure 1¾" (4.5 cm) from the knot and tie another knot. Slide on a multicolored plastic bead, and tie a knot flush against the other side of the bead.

17. Repeat Step 16 another 2 times, then measure 3½" (9 cm) from the last knot. This area will be the center of the necklace. Tie a knot and slide on a multicolored plastic bead. Tie another knot flush against the other side of the bead.

18. Repeat Step 16 another 3 times.

19. Measure 2¾" (7 cm) from the last bead at either end of the cord. Double check the length of the necklace and adjust the length of the cord ends, as desired. Trim the excess cord.

20. Make a ⅙" (4 mm) fold at one end of the cord. Slide on a cord tip and flatten to secure.

21. Repeat Step 20 at the other end of the cord.

22. Open two ⅕" (5 mm) jump rings and slide each one onto a cord tip. String a clasp to one of the jump rings and close the jump rings. (Fig. 4)

23. Open the ⅓" (9 mm) jump ring and string it through the loop at the top of the Lime Drop Pendant. Wrap the jump ring around the gold cord at the center of the necklace and close the jump ring.

Fanciful Fairy Necklace

The pendant features a pretty pink and purple batik pendant that is decorated on the top and bottom with faceted crystal beads, gold beads and an elegant dangling chain. The combination of ribbons creates a delicately distinct piece of jewelry.

MATERIALS

Fanciful Pendant

1 Bristol Board Base (page 20), tie wire still inside, round with a wavy edge, about 2¼" (5.5 cm) diameter

1 sheet of batik paper, variegated pink and purple

Diluted PVA glue

Varnish

1 gold-plated head pin, 2½" (6.4 cm) long

Delicate gold-plated chain, 3½" (9 cm) long

8 small glass beads, various shades of pink, purple, and transparent, 1" (2.5 cm) diameter

2 medium glass beads, different shades of purple, ¼" (6 mm) diameter

11 gold-plated head pins, ¾" (2 cm) long

3 gold-plated jump rings: one ¼" (6 mm) jump ring and two ⅛" (3 mm) jump rings

1 filigree gold-plated bead cap, ¼" (6 mm) diameter

1 large purple glass bead, ⅓" (8 mm) diameter

Neck Ribbon

Gold thread

Pale pink ribbon, 2" (5 cm) wide, about 20" (50 cm) long

Green ribbon, 1" (2.5 cm) wide, about 19½" (49 cm) long

Fuchsia ribbon, 1" (2.5 cm) wide, about 19½" (49 cm) long

2 gold-plated cord tips with connecting rings

3 gold-plated textured tube beads, ¼" (6 mm) inside diameter, ⅓" (9 mm) overall diameter

1 gold-plated clasp

3 gold-plated jump rings: two ¼" (6 mm) jump ring and one ⅛" (3 mm) jump ring

TOOLS

Viewfinder (page 30)	Needle
Pencil	Ruler
Scissors	Wire cutters
Support stand	Round-nose pliers

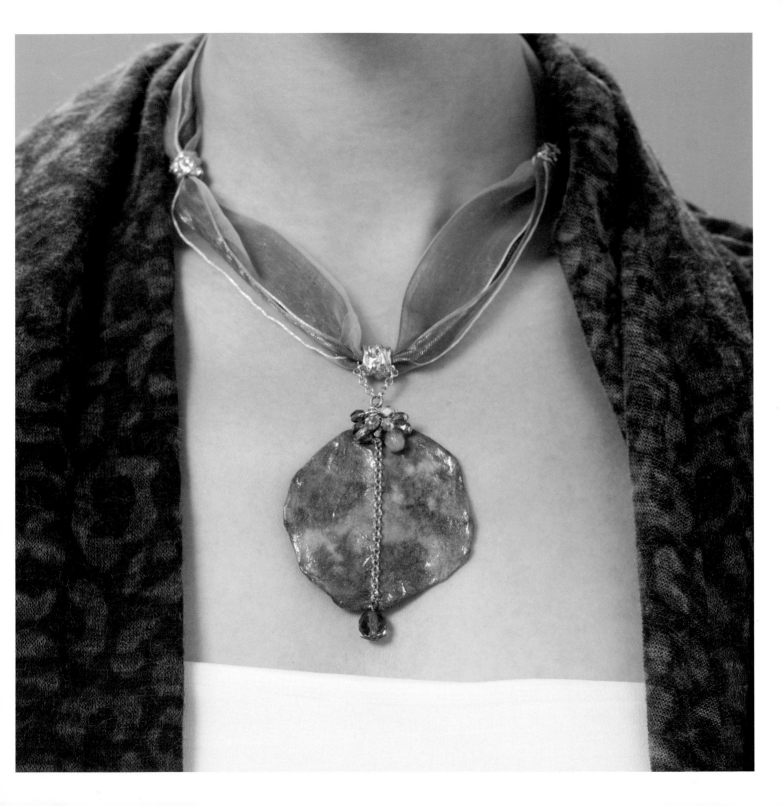

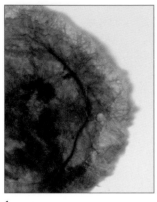

1

2

3

4

DIRECTIONS

Fanciful Pendant

1. Using the viewfinder, find the part of the batik paper you want to use to cover the base. Trace the Bristol Board Base onto the paper, adding a ½" (1.3 cm) margin all around, and cut.

2. Brush diluted PVA glue on one face and around the edge of the base. Position 1 piece of paper on the base and affix. (Fig. 1)

3. Brush diluted PVA glue on the surface of the paper, working from the center outward, and smoothing out air bubbles as you brush. Brush around the edges as well. Let dry for about 5 minutes.

4. Gently tear off the excess paper, leaving only the face and edge covered. Let dry.

5. Repeat Steps 2 to 4 on the other side of the base, brushing around the edges with diluted glue until smooth. Let dry. Brush varnish on both faces of the base and let dry.

6. Carefully remove the tie wire from the base, and insert the gold-plated head pin. Allow ⅓" (9 mm) to extend above the base, then trim the excess wire. Make a loop at the tip.

7. String 1 small glass bead onto 1 small head pin. Allow ⅓" (9 mm) of wire to extend above the bead and trim the excess wire. Make a loop at the tip.

8. Repeat Step 7 with the other small and medium glass beads, for a total of 10 dangling beads

9. Open the ¼" (6 mm) jump ring and string on dangling glass beads in the following order: 1 medium bead, 4 small beads, 1 medium bead and 4 small beads. Close the jump ring. (Fig. 2)

10. String the bead cap and the large glass bead onto a small head pin. Allow ⅓" (9 mm) of the head pin to extend and trim

5   6

the excess wire. Make a loop at the tip, but do not close it. Cut the gold-plated chain into two pieces: one 2" (5 cm) and one 1½" (4 cm). String the last link of the longer chain through the loop and close the loop. (Fig. 3)

11. Open a ⅛" (3 mm) jump ring and insert it through the link at the free end of the longer chain. Draw this jump ring through the jump ring supporting the 10 dangling beads and close the jump ring.

12. Open a ⅛" (3 mm) jump ring, draw it through the loop at the top of the pendant and close the jump ring. Open another ⅛" (3 mm) jump ring. String it through the jump ring attached to the pendant and the jump ring connecting the longer chain and the 10 dangling beads. Close the jump ring.

Neck Ribbon

13. Place the ribbons in a stack, with the pale pink ribbon on the bottom, the green ribbon in the middle and the fuchsia ribbon on top. Center the upper ribbons on the bottom ribbon

and allow the end of the bottom ribbon to extend by about ¼" (6 mm) above the other ribbons.

14. Fold the top edge of the bottom ribbon over the other two ribbons.

15. Fold one side of the folded section toward the center of the ribbon. Fold the other side toward the center, overlapping the first side. Sew the ends together securely. (Fig. 4)

16. Fold the sewn end and slide it into a cord tip. Make sure the ribbon is securely tucked inside; then flatten with the flat-nose pliers

17. Roll the tip of the unfinished end of ribbon until it is narrow enough for sliding on the beads, then gently slide on 3 gold-plated textured tube beads. Position 1 bead 4" (10 cm) from the cord tip, 1 bead at the center of the necklace and 1 bead 4" (10 cm) from the unfinished end.

18. Insert the 1½" (4 cm) piece of gold-plated chain through the center tube bead. Open a ⅛" (3 mm) jump ring and slide it on the first and last links of the chain. Slide on the jump ring at the top of the Fanciful Pendant and close the jump ring. (Fig. 5)

19. Double check the length of the necklace and trim excess ribbon if necessary. Repeat Steps 14 to 16 to fold and sew the other end of the ribbon and tuck it into the cord tip.

20. Open both ⅛" (3 mm) jump rings and insert one into each cord tip. Slide one part of the clasp on each jump ring and close the jump rings. (Fig. 6)

Fuchsia Hoop Earrings

These dazzling earrings feature glittering handmade disks that are set off by textured beads and gold accents. Make the disks as big as your dare, for a show-stopping look.

MATERIALS

Fuchsia Disks

2 Corrugated Cardboard Bases (page 22), tie wire still inside, round, about 1¾" (4.5 cm) diameter

Diluted PVA glue

1 sheet of batik paper, multihued pink, 9 x 12" (21 x 30 cm)

Gold thread

PVA glue

Gold and fuchsia glitter glue

Varnish

Earrings

2 pieces of brass wire, 24-gauge (0.5 mm), each 16" (40 cm) long

8 filigree gold-plated bead caps, about ¼" (6 mm) diameter

4 multihued glittery plastic beads, ⅓" (9 mm) diameter

1 pair of gold-plated ear wires

TOOLS

Viewfinder (page 30)

Paintbrush

Flat-nose pliers

Round-nose pliers

Wire cutters

Support stand

Scissors

Pencil

1   2   3

DIRECTIONS

Fuchsia Disks

1. Using the viewfinder, find the part of the batik paper that you want to use to cover the bases. Trace 4 circles, each with a 2¾" (7 cm) diameter, onto the batik paper and cut out.

2. Brush diluted PVA glue on one face and around the edge of 1 base. Position 1 piece of batik paper onto the base and affix.

3. Brush the surface of the batik paper with diluted PVA glue, working from the center of the base outward, and smoothing out air bubbles as you brush. Brush around the edges as well. Let dry for about 5 minutes.

4. Gently tear off excess paper, leaving only the face and edges covered, and let dry.

5. Repeat Steps 2 to 4 on the other side of the base and let dry. Repeat Steps 2 to 5 to cover the other base.

6. Cut a 32" (80 cm) piece of gold thread. Measure 2" (5 cm) from one end of the thread and place this part of the thread on the bottom of the base. Apply a drop of PVA glue here and press with your finger to affix. Leave both ends of the thread dangling and set aside until the glue dries.

7. Carefully draw the longer end of the thread diagonally upward across the face of the base, holding the starting point with your fingers. Wrap the thread diagonally toward the back of the base, then diagonally toward the front.

8. Continue wrapping the thread diagonally around the base several times.

9. When you're satisfied with the design, tie both ends of the thread together and brush a little PVA glue on the knot. Delicately apply dots of glue at several more spots along the thread until it is securely affixed to the base. Let dry.

10. Repeat Steps 6 to 9 to wrap the other base with gold thread.

11. Apply some glitter glue to both bases, gently spreading it over the front and back using your fingers. Let dry. Brush varnish on both pieces and let dry. Remove the tie wires.

Earrings

12. Make a small loop at 1 end of 1 piece of brass wire. Insert the straight end of the wire through 1 gold-plated bead cap, 1 multihued bead and 1 gold-plated bead cap. Insert the wire into 1 Fuchsia Disk, from the top to the bottom, then slide on 1 gold-plated bead cap, 1 multihued bead and 1 gold-plated bead cap.

13. Make a 90-degree bend in the wire and begin curving it gently upward, in a circle.

14. Draw the wire around one side of the Fuchsia Disk, and through the loop at the top. Continue drawing the wire around the disk, forming a full circle. (Fig. 1)

15. Estimate the size of hoop you want. Allow another ⅓" (9 mm) of wire and then trim the excess wire. Make a loop at the tip, drawing it through the loop at the bottom of the base. Close the loop. (Fig. 2)

16. Open the loop on the ear wire, insert it into the loop at the top of the Fuchsia Disk, and close the loop. (Fig. 3)

17. Repeat Steps 12 to 16 to make the matching earring.

This variation features a rectangular base.

Wistful Wispy Earrings

This design is a perfect example of how scraps of paper and old jewelry components can be combined to create spectacular jewelry pieces. Assorted pieces of washi paper are used to make the paper piece in this design. As for the clip-on earrings, they were salvaged from an old pair of earrings and covered with a piece of delicate pink napkin.

MATERIALS

Wispy Dangling Disks

Small pieces of washi paper, various colors

2 Bristol Board Bases (page 20), tie wire still inside, round with a wavy edge, about 2¼" (5.7 cm) diameter

Diluted PVA glue

Gold Dust Mixture (page 40)

Varnish

Earrings

32 gold-plated head pins: two 2½" (6.4 cm) long and thirty ¾" (2 cm) long

2 pieces of gold-plated box chain, each 3" (7.6 cm) long

12 gold-plated jump rings: ten ⅕" (5 mm) jump rings and two ⅜" (1 cm) jump rings

30 multifaceted crystal beads, various shades of pink and purple, ¼" (6 mm)

1 pair decorated clip-on earrings, with 1 hole

TOOLS

Paintbrushes

Wire cutters

Round-nose pliers

Flat-nose pliers

Support stand

1   2   3   4

DIRECTIONS

Wispy Dangling Disks

1. Tear the washi paper into small pieces. (Fig. 1)

2. Brush diluted PVA glue on the face and sides of 1 base.

3. Brush diluted PVA glue on both sides of a small piece of washi paper and affix to the base. Rub the paper lightly after it has been affixed, either with your fingertips or a paintbrush, to remove air bubbles and fasten it securely to the shape.

4. Repeat Step 3 to create a colorful washi carpet on one side of the base. Make sure to cover the edges of the piece as well by wrapping pieces of paper from the front to the back. Brush diluted PVA glue all around the edges to affix the papers. Let dry. (Fig. 2)

5. Repeat Steps 2 to 4 to cover the other face of this base, then repeat to cover both sides of the other base.

6. Dip a paintbrush in gold dust mixture and tap the mixture on both sides of both pieces. Let dry. Brush varnish all over both pieces and let dry. Carefully remove the tie wires.

Earrings

7. Insert a 2½" (6.4 cm) head pin through the tunnel in 1 Wispy Dangling Disk. Allow ⅓" (9 mm) of wire to extend above the base; then trim the excess wire. Form a loop at the tip but don't close the loop.

8. Repeat Step 7 with the other disk.

9. Cut 1 gold-plated chain into 2 pieces: one ½" (1.3 cm) long and one 2½" (6.4 cm) long. Open a ⅕" (5 mm) jump ring and draw it through the links at one end of both chains. Do not close the jump ring.

5 6 7

10. String a crystal bead onto a ¾" (2 cm) long head pin. Allow ⅓" (9 mm) of wire to extend from the bead; then trim the excess wire. Form a loop at the tip. (Fig. 3)

11. Repeat Step 10 to make 15 dangling crystal beads.

12. Open three ⅕" (5 mm) jump rings. String 6 dangling beads on 1 jump ring; 5 dangling beads on another jump ring; and 3 dangling beads on the third jump ring. Close the jump rings. (Fig. 4)

13. Open a ⅜" (1 cm) jump ring, string it through the 3 jump rings from Step 12 and close the jump ring. (Fig. 5)

14. Draw the jump ring connecting the two chains through the hole in the clip-on earring. (Fig. 6) String on the jump ring with the dangling beads and make sure the chains hang behind the beads. Close the jump ring.

15. Open a ⅕" (5 mm) jump ring and string it through the loop of 1 dangling bead and the bottom link of the long chain. Close the jump ring. (Fig. 7)

16. String the bottom link in the short piece of chain onto the open loop on top of the Wispy Dangling Disk. Close the loop.

17. Repeat Steps 9 to 16 to make the matching earring.

Orange Globe Earrings

These earrings have an element of ancient beauty to them. Streamlined yet dramatic, they are excellent for daily wear. Follow these basic steps using any selection of handmade and store-bought beads.

MATERIALS

Orange Globe Beads

1 sheet of washi paper, orange, 6 x 6" (15 x 15 cm)

2 round beads, ¾" (2 cm) diameter

Tie wire, 19-gauge (0.9 mm), 16" (40 cm)

Diluted PVA glue

Gold Dust Mixture (page 40)

Varnish

Earrings

2 pieces of gold-plated rope chain, each 3" (7.6 cm) long

2 gold-plated crimp beads

2 large gold-plated beads, ¼" (6 mm) diameter

2 patterned silver-colored beads, ¼ x ½" (0.6 x 1.3 cm)

4 filigree gold-plated bead caps, ¼" (6 mm) diameter

2 small gold-plated beads, ⅛" (3 mm) diameter

2 gold-plated eye pins, 2" (5 cm) long

1 pair of gold-plated ear wires

TOOLS

Paintbrushes

Wire cutters

Flat-nose pliers

Round-nose pliers

Ruler

Support stand

1   2   3   4

DIRECTIONS

Orange Globe Beads

1. Tear 2 strips of washi paper that are long enough to wrap around each round bead, and provide a ½" (1.3 cm) margin for gluing. Make sure the strips are wide enough to cover the bead diameter as well.

2. Cut 2 pieces of tie wire, each about 8" (20 cm) long. Insert each wire into a bead and position the bead in the middle of the wire. Bend the wire on either side of the bead to make a U shape. This wire supports the bead as you proceed.

3. Brush diluted PVA glue over 1 bead. Affix 1 piece of washi paper by pressing an edge of the paper onto the bead. Wrap the paper around the bead while brushing it with diluted PVA glue. The texture will likely be a bit wrinkly. Press the surface gently, either with the paintbrush or your fingertips, as you wrap. (Fig. 1)

4. Let the bead dry for a bit, then make adjustments to the surface by pressing and smoothing it with your fingertips. Make sure the washi paper is firmly attached to the bead. Brush with a bit more diluted PVA glue, if necessary, and smooth out air bubbles. Let dry. (Fig. 2)

5. Repeat Steps 3 and 4 with the other bead.

6. Dip a paintbrush in gold dust mixture, and trickle droplets on the surface of the beads. Allow the mixture to pool randomly, giving the beads a metallic look. Brush varnish all over the beads and let dry. Carefully remove the tie wires.

Earrings

7. Fold 1 chain in half and slide the ends into a crimp bead. Draw the crimp bead up toward the folded end of the chain, creating a small loop at that end. Flatten the crimp bead with flat-nose pliers.

8. String 1 large gold-plated bead, 1 patterned silver-colored bead, 1 gold-plated bead cap, 1 Orange Globe Bead, 1 gold-plated bead cap and 1 small gold-plated bead onto an eye pin. Allow about ⅓" (9 mm) of wire to extend above the top bead and trim the excess wire. Make a loop at the tip. Do not close the loop.

9. Draw the loop you formed in the chain through the open loop in the eye pin, then close the loop in the eye pin. (Fig. 3)

10. Open the loop at the bottom of 1 ear wire and string it onto the loop at the top of the decorated eye pin. Close the loop. (Fig. 4)

11. Repeat Steps 7 to 10 to make the matching earring.

This variation features a gold-and-black paper ball framed by rhinestone-inlaid components.

Swinging Triangle Earrings

These geometric earrings feature a combination of balsa wood strips, nickel wire and colorful origami paper. Lighthearted and distinct, you'll feel as if you have tiny pieces of artwork dangling from your ears.

MATERIALS

1 strip of balsa wood, ⅛ x ⅛ x 6" (0.4 x 0.4 x 15 cm)

Nickel silver wire, 24-gauge (0.5 mm), 15¾" (40 cm) long

1 sheet of origami paper, 6 x 6" (15 x 15 cm)

PVA glue

2 nickel silver jump rings, ⅛" (3 mm)

1 pair of thin nickel-plated ear wires

TOOLS

Utility knife

Cutting mat

Ruler

Pencil

Round-nose pliers

Wire cutters

Flat-nose pliers

Scissors

Paintbrush

1   2   3   4

DIRECTIONS

1. Bevel one end of the balsa wood strip at a 45-degree angle with the utility knife. Measure 2" (5 cm) along the strip and bevel the other end. (Fig. 1)

2. Cut an 8" (20 cm) piece of nickel silver wire. Grasp the wire with the tip of the round-nose pliers, about ⅙" (4 mm) from the end, and make a 90-degree bend in the wire. Measure another ⅙" (4 mm) along the wire and make another 90-degree bend. Repeat one more time to form a square of wire that fits over one end of the beveled strip.

3. Measure 1⅞" (4.7 cm) from the bottom of the square and make a 45-degree bend in the wire, forming an isosceles triangle.

4. Measure 1⅞" (4.7) from the top of the triangle, grasp the wire with the round-nose pliers and make a 90-degree bend. Measure another ⅙" (4 mm) along the wire, and make another 90-degree bend. Repeat one more time to form an identical square at the other end of the wire. Cut the excess wire and reserve for Step 6. (Fig. 2)

5. Slide each end of the wood strip through a wire square, and secure the wire in place by pressing gently with the flat-nose pliers. (Fig. 3)

6. Repeat Steps 1 to 5 to make the triangular base for the second earring.

7. Cut two 2" (5 cm) pieces of nickel silver wire. Make a loop at one end of each piece of wire. Do not close the loop. Make sure that the rods you've made are a bit shorter than the height of the triangle.

5   6   7

8. Draw 2 strips, each about ½" (1.3 cm) wide, on the back of the origami paper and cut. Measure 1½" (4 cm) and cut, then measure another ¾" (2 cm) and cut. You'll now have 2 pairs of rectangles, one set for each earring.

9. Fold 1 larger rectangle in half, undecorated sides together. Brush PVA glue on the undecorated sides of the paper, then slip the straight end of 1 wire rod from Step 7 between the glued sides of the paper. Make sure the wire is sandwiched directly in the middle of the paper. Press the sides together to affix. Let dry. (Fig. 4)

10. Brush PVA glue on the undecorated side of the smaller rectangle and wrap it around the center of 1 wooden strip. Let dry. (Fig. 5)

11. String the top of the wire triangle through the loop at the top of the wire rod. Slide a jump ring onto the loop, then close the loop. (Fig. 6)

12. Open the loop at the bottom of the ear wire and string it through the jump ring. Close the loop. (Fig. 7)

13. Repeat Steps 9 to 12 to make the matching earring.

Violet Night Earrings

The paper base in this design is made by combining two base-making techniques. The base is first made with Bristol board, then the contours are built up with paper pulp. It is decorated with vibrant silver, gold, fuchsia and violet paint and just the right amount of glitter for a truly inspired design.

MATERIALS

Violet Night Beads

2 sheets of Bristol board, 3 x 6" (7 x 15 cm)

Tie wire, 19-gauge (0.9 mm)

PVA glue

Paper pulp (page 19)

Purple, fuchsia and blue acrylic paints

Water

Fuchsia, gold and silver glitter glue

Gloss glaze

Earrings

Delicate gold-plated chain, 7½" (19 cm) long

Delicate silver-plated chain, 3" (8 cm) long

2 gold-plated head pins, 2" (5 cm) long

2 gold-plated jump rings, ⅕" (5 mm)

4 brass jump rings: two ⅓" (9 mm) jump rings and two ⅕" (5 mm) jump rings

1 pair of gold-plated lever-back ear wires, with loops

2 antique-style gold-plated rings, about ½" (1.3 cm) diameter

TOOLS

Pencil

Scissors

Paintbrushes

Support stand

Plastic container for storing paper pulp

Plastic container for mixing paint

Wire cutters

Round-nose pliers

1

2

3

4

DIRECTIONS

Violet Night Beads

1. Fold 1 sheet of Bristol board in half and draw an abstract shape measuring about ½ x 2" (4 x 5 cm). Cut out the shape to make 2 identical shapes.

2. Fold the other sheet of Bristol board in half, trace the shape from Step 1 and cut out. You should now have 4 identical shapes. Follow directions for making and covering a Bristol Board Base (page 20). (Fig. 1)

3. Spread a thin layer of PVA glue on one face of one base. Spread a thin coating of paper pulp with your fingers. Tap gently and smooth with a glue-covered finger or paintbrush until completely covered. Let dry.

4. Repeat Step 3 on one face of the other Bristol board shape and then on the reverse faces of both bases.

NOTE Store the paper pulp in a covered container in the refrigerator as you wait for the base to dry between stages.

5. Place a bit of each paint color in a plastic container. Mix some of the paints together for a variety of shades. Dilute some of the paint with water for a variety of consistencies (page 39).

6. Tap each base lightly at different spots, using different shades of paints, until you achieve the desired result. Apply a darker shade along the edges. Let dry. (Fig. 2)

7. Paint the back of each piece as well. Let dry. Brush glitter glue randomly and delicately on both sides of both pieces. (Fig. 3)

8. Brush gloss glaze on both sides of both pieces and let dry. Carefully remove the tie wires from the bases.

5 6 7

Earrings

9. Insert a head pin through the tunnel in each Violet Night Bead. Allow ⅓" (9 mm) of wire to extend and trim the excess wire. Make a loop at the tip that is aligned with the piece and close the loop. (Fig. 4)

10. Cut the gold-plated chain in half, then cut each half into two uneven sections. Cut the silver-plated chain in half.

11. Open 1 gold-plated jump ring and string on 1 short gold-plated chain, 1 silver-plated chain and 1 long gold-plated chain. Don't close the jump ring. (Fig. 5)

12. Draw the loop on one Violet Night Bead onto the jump ring. Close the jump ring.

13. Open a ⅓" (9 mm) brass jump ring, insert it through the loop of 1 ear wire and close the jump ring. (Fig. 6)

14. Open a ⅕" (5 mm) brass jump ring and draw it through the ⅓" (9 mm) brass jump ring and 1 antique gold-plated ring. Draw the jump ring through the loop at the top of the bead and close the jump ring. (Fig. 7)

15. Repeat Steps 11 to 15 to make the matching earring.

Origami Chime Brooch

This imaginative brooch combines several techniques and diverse materials. The origami paper is highlighted in the triangular base at the top and the eight delicate chimes that dangle from the base.

MATERIALS

Triangular Base

Corrugated cardboard

PVA glue

Computer paper or newspaper, straight edges torn away

Diluted PVA glue

1 sheet of origami paper

Black acrylic paint

1 gold-plated pin back

Jewelry adhesive

Black paper, 2 x 2" (5 x 5 cm)

Varnish

Origami-Covered Wood Rods

Wood rod, ⅙" (4 mm) diameter, 16" (40 cm) long

Sandpaper

PVA glue

Nickel silver wire, 26-gauge (0.4 mm), 80" (203 cm) long

8 brass jump rings, 5/16" (7 mm) each

TOOLS

Utility knife

Cutting mat

Sandpaper

Paintbrushes

Ruler

Needle

Small saw, optional

Round-nose pliers

Flat-nose pliers

Wire cutters

Pencil

1   2   3   4

DIRECTIONS

Triangular Base

1. Trace Drawing 1 and Drawing 2 (page 127) onto corrugated cardboard and cut.

2. Brush PVA glue on the back of the smaller triangle. Position this triangle on top of the larger triangle, so that the margins at the sides are even and the margin at the bottom is larger. Press the smaller triangle onto the larger one to affix. Let dry. (Fig. 1)

3. Follow directions for covering a Corrugated Cardboard Base (page 22) and cover the stacked triangles with 1 or 2 layers of paper. Let dry.

4. Mark 8 dots along the bottom of the larger triangle, at equal distance from the edges and from each other. Pierce a hole at each dot with the needle. (Fig. 2)

5. Trace Drawing 2 (page 127) onto the origami paper, and cut. Reserve the excess paper for decorating the wood rods.

6. Brush PVA glue on the top of the smaller triangle of the base and affix the origami triangle on top. Let dry.

7. Paint the rest of the base with black paint. Make sure the paint reaches the 8 holes along the base, but make sure they aren't filled with paint. Carefully paint the sides of the smaller triangle and the edges of the origami-covered face, creating a black contour. Let dry. (Fig. 3)

NOTE PVA glue may sometimes reject acrylic paint. If necessary, apply a second coat of paint to cover up any unsealed spots.

8. Apply jewelry adhesive to the back of the pin back and affix to the back of the larger triangle, at the center. Conceal the flat part of the pin back by affixing a small piece of black paper over top. Let dry.

5   6

9. Brush varnish on all sides of the piece, taking care not to cover the pin's apparatus. Let dry.

Origami-Covered Wood Rods

10. Draw 8 rectangles on the reserved origami paper, each measuring about 1¼ x ¾" (3.2 x 1.9 cm), and cut. Cut the wood rod into 8 sections, varying in length between 1½" (4 cm) to 2" (5 cm). If you are using a utility knife, cut the wood by rotating the knife around the strip. If you have a small saw, simply saw gently through the strip. Rub sandpaper on the ends of each wooden strip until smooth.

11. Spread PVA glue along one narrow edge of an origami paper rectangle. Attach a corner of the rectangle to a rod, at an angle, and wrap around the rod. Brush PVA glue on the top to affix. (Fig. 4)

12. Repeat Step 11 to cover the other rods with the origami paper rectangles.

13. Cut 8 pieces of nickel wire, each measuring about 10" (25 cm).

14. Using the round-nose pliers, form a tight 3-rotation coil at the tip of 1 piece of nickel wire. Slide the coils onto the bottom of 1 origami-covered rod, with the straight end of wire extending upward.

15. Make 3 rotations in the wire as you twist it toward the top of the rod, pulling firmly to tighten it. (Fig. 5)

16. Make 3 tightly coiled rotations at the top of the rod, to secure the wire.

17. Using the round-nose pliers, bend the wires at a 90-degree angle. Make a tight double loop at the top of the wire, and trim the excess wire. (Fig. 6)

18. Repeat Steps 14 to 17 to coil the other wires. Open the jump rings and insert each one into a hole on the triangular base. Draw each jump ring through the loop at the top of a rod and close the jump ring.

This variation features a rectangular base and includes green paint that highlights the origami paper.

Glittery Batik Paper Brooch

❦

This striking brooch can be assembled using any combination of decorative papers you like. It's a great platform for showing off a small piece of paper, such as a scrap of wallpaper. You can cut the base pieces in any size and shape. Use an assortment of glitter glues to produce a profusion of color.

MATERIALS

Corrugated cardboard

Computer paper or newspaper, straight edges torn away

Diluted PVA glue

2 sheets of batik paper, green and purple, 9 x 12" (21 x 30 cm)

Gold paper, 2 x 2" (5 x 5 cm)

PVA glue

Varnish

1 gold-plated pin back

Jewelry adhesive

Gold and purple glitter glue

TOOLS

Pencil

Utility knife

Cutting mat

Paintbrushes

Scissors

 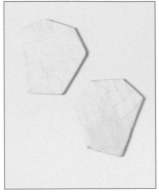  

1   2   3   4

DIRECTIONS

1. Trace Drawing 1 (page 127) twice onto corrugated cardboard and cut out. (Fig. 1)

2. Follow directions for preparing 2 Corrugated Cardboard Bases (page 22) and cover each base with 1 layer of paper. (Fig. 2)

3. Trace Drawing 1 onto a piece of batik paper. Add a ½" (1.3 cm) border all around and cut out. Repeat with the other piece of batik paper.

4. Spread diluted PVA glue on one cardboard base. Position one piece of batik paper on top and affix.

5. Working from the center toward the edge, brush diluted PVA glue across the top of the batik paper, smoothing out air bubbles as you brush. Brush around the edges as well to affix the paper all around. Let dry.

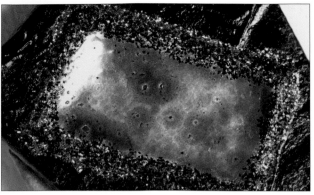

5

6

6. Turn over the base and fold the edges of the batik paper toward the center. Working from the edges inward, brush with diluted PVA glue until the surface is smooth. Let dry. (Fig. 3)

7. Repeat Steps 4 to 6 to cover the other cardboard base. Brush varnish on both sides of each base and let dry.

8. Trace Drawing 2 (page 127) onto the gold paper and cut out. Position the paper on the top piece of the brooch and affix with PVA glue. Let dry. (Fig. 4)

9. Apply a border of gold and purple glitter glue around the gold paper. (Fig. 5)

10. Position the pin back on the back of the bottom piece of the brooch and affix with jewelry adhesive. Let dry. Conceal

the flat part of the pin back by affixing a small piece of batik paper and let dry. Cover with varnish, taking care not to cover the pin's apparatus, and let dry.

11. Arrange the front and back pieces of the brooch as desired, and affix with PVA glue. Let dry. (Fig. 6)

Delicate Maidenhair Leaf Brooch

The washi paper in this brooch was the inspiration for its design. The paper's delicate leaf shapes, similar to those found on the maidenhair, or ginkgo, tree, merited a lovely, delicate piece of jewelry.

MATERIALS

Piece of thick handmade paper, cream colored, 9 x 12" (21 x 30 cm)

Piece of washi paper, decorated with leaves, 9 x 12" (21 x 30 cm)

Piece of washi paper, gold-printed, 1 x 1" (2.5 x 2.5 cm)

Plastic wrap

Transparent fabric hardener

1 gold-plated pin back

PVA glue

TOOLS

Pencil

Cutting mat

Utility knife

Paintbrushes

Scissors

1

2

3

DIRECTIONS

1. Trace Drawing 1 and Drawing 2 (page 126) on the thick handmade paper and cut out. Trace Drawing 3 (page 126) on the decorated washi paper and cut out. Trace Drawing 4 (page 126) on the gold-printed washi paper, and cut out. These become Cuttings 1, 2, 3 and 4.

2. Line your work surface with plastic wrap and place all 4 pieces of paper on top. Brush fabric hardener on one side of each piece. Let dry.

3. Turn the papers over and apply fabric hardener to the other side of each piece. Let dry.

4. Fold the sides of Cutting 1 (see drawing). Since the paper has stiffened, it will hold the folds. (Fig. 1)

5. Fold Cutting 2 into fanlike accordion pleats that are wide at the top and narrow at the bottom. (Fig. 2)

4

5

6. Make small X-shaped cuts on Cutting 3 (see drawing). Press the pin back onto the cutting so that the protruding areas and the pin extend out the back. (Fig. 3)

7. Spread PVA glue on the back of Cutting 3, taking care not to cover the pin's apparatus. Affix Cutting 3 onto the back of Cutting 1, sandwiching the flat part of the pin between the two cuttings. Hold together to affix, then set aside to dry.

8. Spread a little PVA glue inside Cutting 1, at the bottom, and on the back of one free flap of Cutting 2. Position the flap next to the fold on the inner side of Cutting 1. Hold the two pieces together until affixed. Repeat with the free flap at the other side. Flatten the bottom of the fan a little, and press tightly against the back. (Fig. 4)

9. Spread PVA glue on Cutting 4 and fold it over the bottom of the fan, so that the triangular end of the paper is visible on the front of the brooch. Hold together until dry. (Fig. 5)

Make a variety of fan brooches using fine paper, delicate beads and your imagination.

Japanese Peacock Brooch

🐚

Some decorated papers feature a solid side and a decorated side. In this project, both sides of a single piece of paper are displayed, for maximum effect. A textured gold tube bead makes a dramatic finish and harmonizes perfectly with the paper.

MATERIALS

1 sheet of washi paper, decorative front and black back, 9 x 12" (21 x 30 cm)

Plastic wrap

Transparent fabric hardener

PVA glue

Gold-plated tube bead, ¼" (6 mm) inner diameter, ⅔" (1.5 cm) long

1 gold-plated pin back

Jewelry adhesive

TOOLS

Ruler

Pencil

Paintbrushes

Scissors

Utility knife

Cutting mat

1   2   3

DIRECTIONS

1. Draw 2 rectangles onto the washi paper, in the following dimensions: 2¾ x 6½" (7 x 15 cm) and 2½ x 6" (6.4 x 15 cm). Cut out the rectangles.

2. Line your work surface with plastic wrap and place both rectangles on top, black side up. Brush fabric hardener on black side of each paper. Let dry.

3. Turn the small rectangle over and brush fabric hardener on the other side. Let dry.

4. Place the larger rectangle with the decorative side facing up, and make widthwise accordion folds every 5/16" (7 mm). Fold until you have 8 pointed edges with 16 sides, plus 1 free flap. Position the free flap on the right side of the rectangle. Trim the excess paper. (Fig. 1)

5. Brush PVA glue on the free flap and glue it to the adjacent side. Press gently to affix. (Fig. 2)

6. Brush PVA glue on the back of the last pleat on the left side and glue it to the adjacent pleat. Spread the rest of the pleats open.

7. Place the smaller rectangle with the black side facing up, and make lengthwise accordion folds every 5/16" (7 mm). Fold until you have 7 pointed edges with 14 sides, plus 1 free flap. Position the free flap on the left side of the rectangle. Trim the excess paper and reserve for later.

8. Brush PVA glue on the free flap and affix it to the adjacent side. Press gently to affix.

9. Brush PVA glue on the back of the last pleat on the right side and glue it to the adjacent pleat. Spread the rest of the pleats open. (Fig. 3)

4   5   6

10. Brush PVA glue on the thicker pleats of both rectangles. Place the larger and smaller rectangles side by side, thicker pleats adjacent and bottoms aligned. Hold the thicker pleats together to affix. Let dry. (Fig. 4)

11. Shape the glued rectangles into a fan by grasping the bottom together with one hand, while fanning out the top with your other hand. Make the bottom of the fan smaller by shaving it down with the utility knife in a downward diagonal direction.

12. When the bottom of the fan is the right size, brush it all around with jewelry adhesive, and insert it gently into the tube bead. (Fig. 5)

13. Draw a 1½ x ¾" (4 x 2 cm) rectangle on the reserved washi paper and cut. Place the pin back on the rectangle and mark the location of its protruding ends. Make X-shape cuts in the marked areas.

14. Press the pin back onto the back of the rectangle, allowing the protruding ends and the pin to extend out the back. (Fig. 6)

15. Apply PVA glue to the back of the rectangular piece, including the base of the pin back, and affix onto the back of the brooch at the center. Make sure the glue does not cover the pin's apparatus. Hold together to affix, then set aside to dry.

Deco Sundae Brooch

Combining thick and thin handmade paper creates a design of harmonious contrasts. In this brooch, thin light pink paper is twirled into a cone and affixed to a flat fan-shaped piece of thick gray paper. Assorted beads accent the cone on either side for a design that is delicate and distinct.

MATERIALS

1 sheet of thick handmade paper, variegated gray, 9 x 12" (21 x 30 cm)

1 sheet of thin handmade paper, light pink with embroidery, 9 x 12" (21 x 30 cm)

Plastic wrap

Transparent fabric hardener

PVA glue

Nickel silver wire, 19-gauge (0.9 mm), 4" (10 cm) long

4 glass beads, ¼" (6 mm) diameter

4 pearl beads, ⅙" (4 mm) diameter

4 gold-plated beads, ⅛" (3 mm) diameter

Nickel silver wire, 26-gauge (0.4 mm), 16" (40 cm) long

1 gold-plated pin back

TOOLS

Pencil

Scissors or utility knife

Cutting mat

Paintbrushes

Metalwork file

Round-nose pliers

Wire cutters

Ruler

Flat-nose pliers

Needle

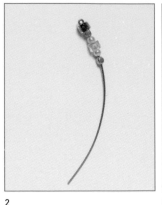

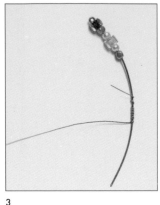

1   2   3   4

DIRECTIONS

1. Trace Drawing 1 and Drawing 3 (page 127) onto the thick handmade paper and cut out. Trace Drawing 2 (page 127) onto the thin handmade paper and cut out. These become Cuttings 1, 2 and 3.

2. Spread plastic wrap on your work area and arrange the cuttings on top. Brush fabric hardener on one side of each cutting and set aside to dry for about 15 minutes.

3. Brush fabric hardener on the other side of each cutting and set aside to dry for about 30 minutes.

4. Bend Cutting 2 into a cone shape and set aside until completely dry. (Fig. 1)

5. Make a ⅛" (3 mm) fold backwards along the edges of Cutting 1, as if you are making a small hem. Brush a bit of PVA glue on the folded area and press gently to affix.

6. File down one end of the thicker wire until smooth and form a loop at the tip. Make a slight curve in the straight part of the wire.

7. Divide the beads into two identical groups and string one of the groups onto the wire in any order you like. Draw the beads up to the loop. (Fig. 2)

8. Cut the thinner wire in half. Wrap 1 half around the thicker wire for about 10 revolutions. (Fig. 3)

9. Leave a 2½" (6.4 cm) tail at one end of the coiled wire and trim the excess wire at the other end. Squeeze the coils together with the flat-nose pliers and draw the coils up to the beads. (Fig. 4)

10. Wrap the other half of the thinner wire in the same manner, then slip the coiled wire off the thicker wire and set aside.

11. Using a needle, gently pierce 1 hole on either side of the

5

6

7

cone, about 1" (2.5 cm) from the bottom and ⅛" (4 mm) from the seam at the back of the cone.

12. Insert the free end of the thicker wire through both holes, drawing the cone onto the wire until it is flush with the coiled wire. (Fig. 5)

13. Slide the coiled you set aside in Step 10 onto the thicker wire, drawing the wire up to the cone. Slide on the remaining beads in the opposite order of the beads strung in Step 7.

14. Allow ⅓" (9 mm) of wire to extend at this end of the thick wire. Cut off the excess and make a loop at the end. Place the decorated cone on top of Cutting 1, and position the two straight ends of thinner wires on top of the cutting. (Fig. 6)

15. Pierce two holes in the cutting exactly where the straight wires touch, then insert the wires through the holes. Twist the wire ends together at the back of the cutting, flatten the wires with the flat-nose pliers and cut the excess wire. (Fig. 7)

16. Make small X-shaped cuts on Cutting 3 (see drawing). Press the pin back onto the cutting so that the protruding areas and the pin extend out the back.

17. Spread PVA glue on the back of Cutting 3, taking care not to cover the pin's apparatus. Affix Cutting 3 onto the back of Cutting 1, sandwiching the flat part of the pin and the twisted wires between the two cuttings. Hold the papers together to affix, then set aside to dry.

In this variation, a playful piece of origami paper is used to make the cone.

DRAWINGS

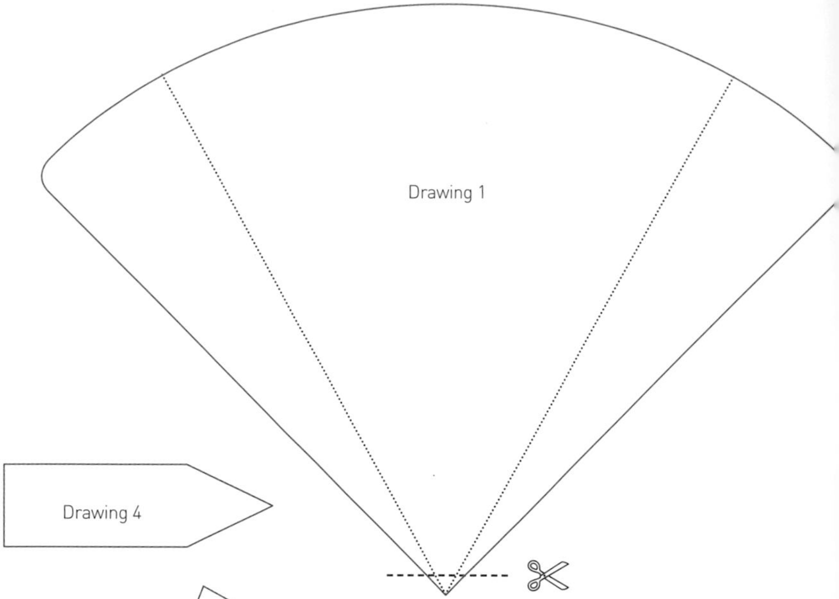

Drawing 1

Drawing 4

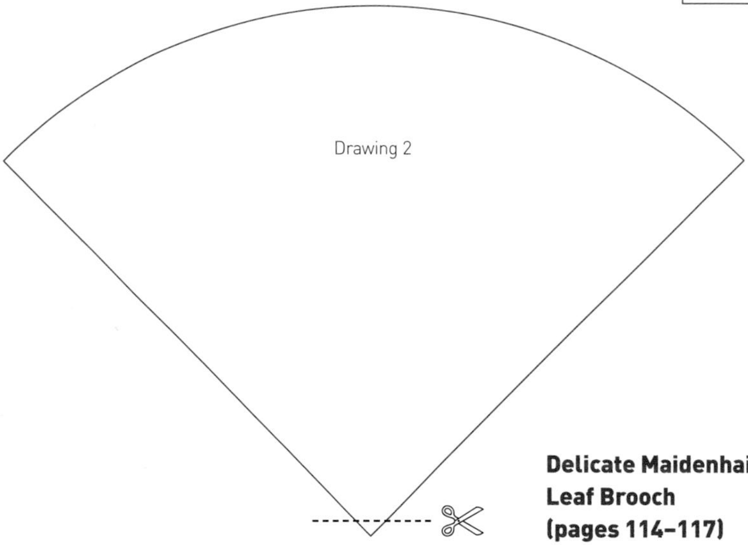

Drawing 2

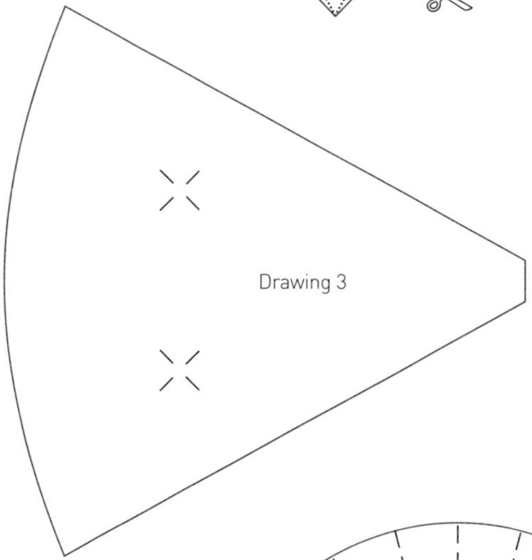

Drawing 3

**Delicate Maidenhair
Leaf Brooch
(pages 114–117)**

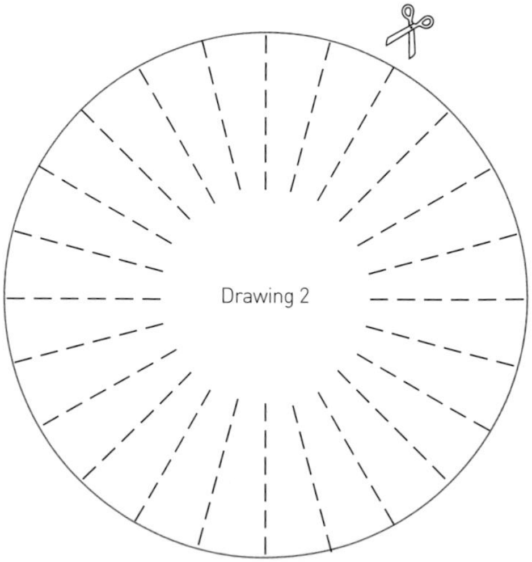

Vanity Flair Necklace (pages 60–64)

Drawing 1

Drawing 2

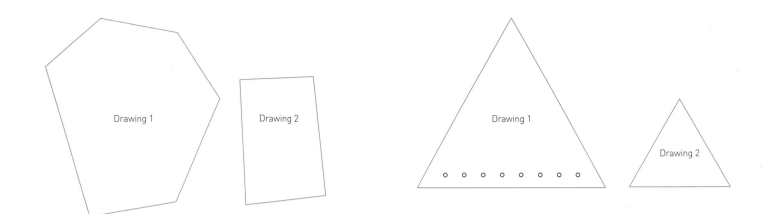

Glittery Batik Paper Brooch (pages 110–113)

Origami Chime Brooch

Drawing 1 — *(triangle with row of circles)*
Drawing 2

Origami Chime Brooch (pages 106–109)

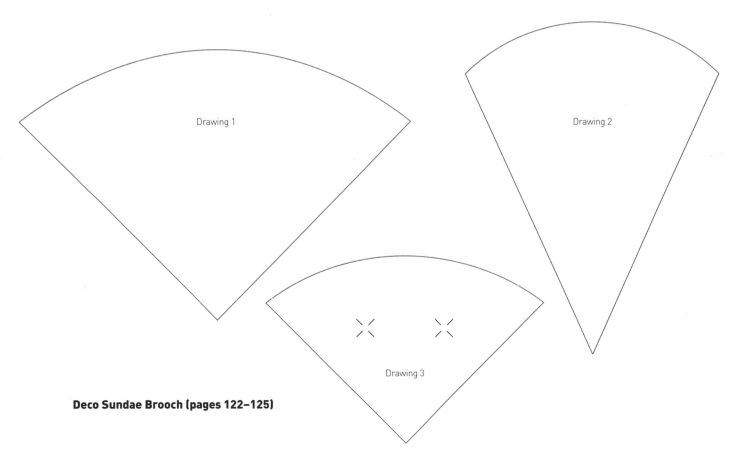

Drawing 1

Drawing 2

Drawing 3

Deco Sundae Brooch (pages 122–125)

INDEX